Gabriele Lehmann-Th.

# WALLPAPER

# WALLPAPER

**PaRragon**

Bath · New York · Singapore · Hong Kong · Cologne · Delhi · Melbourne

This is a Parragon Publishing book
Copyright © Parragon Books Ltd
Parragon Books Ltd
Queen Street House
4 Queen Street
Bath BA1 1HE, UK


Author: Alejandro Asensio
Introduction: Francesc Zamora
Artistic editor: Marta Navarro
Photographic documentation: Javier Alonso
Design and layout: Sigrid Bueno

Copyright © 2007 Parragon Books Ltd for the US edition

US edition produced by Cambridge Publishing Management Ltd
Translation: Leslie Ray
Copy-editing: Sandra Stafford

ISBN 978-1-4054-9304-8

Printed in China

# Contents

# Introduction

In the early 18th century, wallpaper was a costly decorative material that often needed to be acquired through booksellers or merchants specializing in luxury items. Even so, it became an alternative to other techniques for covering walls that were even more expensive, such as the use of sumptuous leathers, silks, wool, or even velvet. England was the most important supplier of wallpaper, but the French, who used more sophisticated techniques, soon overtook their neighbor and dominated the market for most of the 19th century. With industrialization, the continuous evolution in techniques offered faster and less costly production.

Early wallpaper used brightly colored floral designs. Later, this evolved into designs using architectural motifs that decorated the stairwells and large living rooms of stately homes. Far-off and exotic cultures had a major influence on wallpaper. The first wallpapers to arrive in Europe were from China during the 18th century. The designs were executed by hand and represented everyday scenes and occupations, incorporating elements such as birds, flowers, human figures, and trees. Subsequently, the move toward flat forms with clearly defined outlines and circular, rectangular, and square compositions with exotic motifs revealed a Japanese influence.

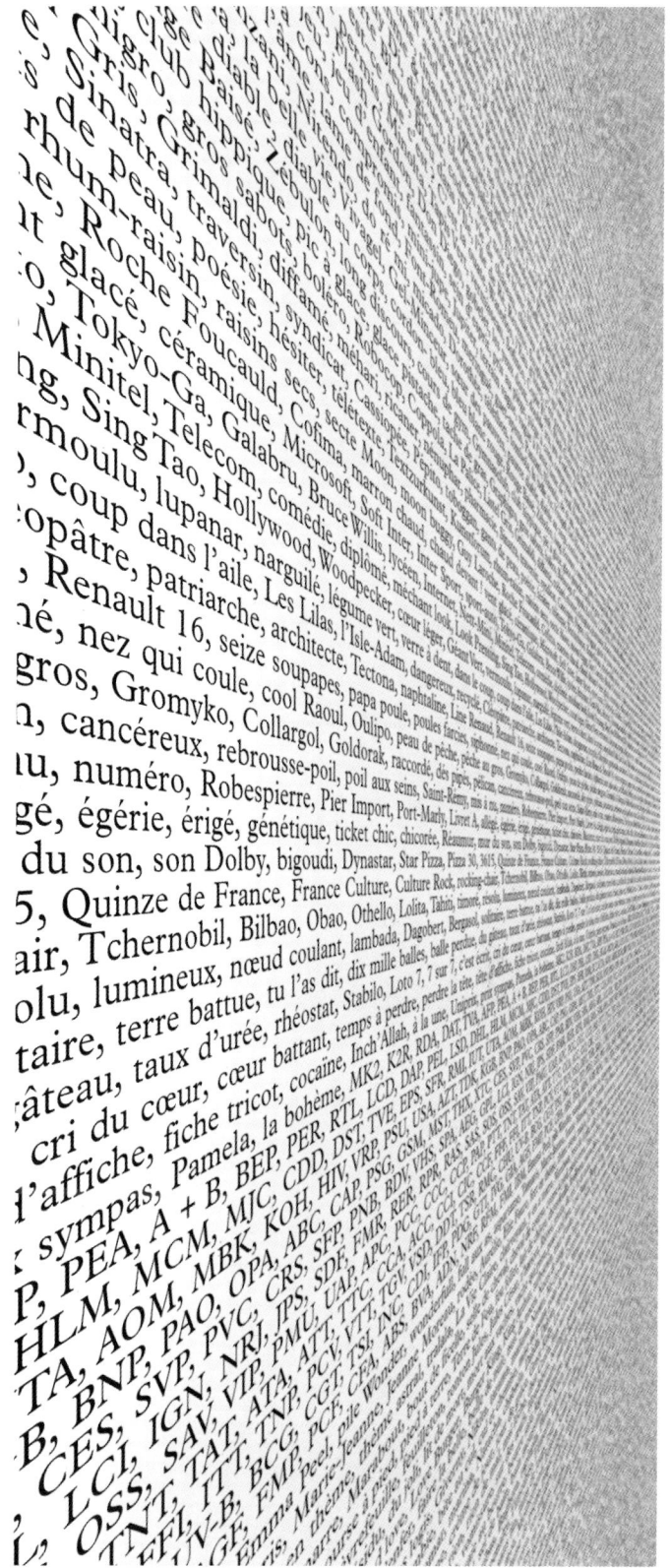

The relationship with the architectural space also became increasingly evident, and excessively ornamental designs were progressively replaced by geometric patterns.

During the final decades of the 19th century, numerous changes occurred in the use and production of wallpaper, which coincided with increased interest in embellishing surfaces. This prompted the manufacturers to create designs for specific spaces in the home. Wallpaper was no longer the domain of the privileged few, and new production methods appeared to create imitations of the embossed and decorated leathers that had been so popular in earlier times. Later, these were turned into embossed papers.

The variety of wallpapers and styles gradually expanded from geometric and abstract patterns that combined with the style of the home to more modern designs created on embossed papers or those with stylized motifs.

New materials were gradually introduced, and vinyl paper began to occupy an important place in commercial and industrial environments. Thanks to its durability and ease of cleaning, it was frequently used to cover surfaces in hospitals, hotels, and restaurants.

These days, the industry continues to develop and reproduce originals of great quality with designs that are strongly rooted in tradition yet reinterpreted to suit the current style.

Damasks have gained increasing popularity, and floral motifs have been reproduced with fascinating ranges of colors and eccentric designs reminiscent of the Op Art of the 1960s and 70s. There is no doubt that wallpaper can change the appearance of a space to an astonishing degree. The key to choosing wallpaper in a contemporary environment lies not so much in knowing how to pick the design as in evaluating its use. For instance, papering a single wall in a room so as not to overload the space, choosing a neutral design to emphasize the elegant lines of furniture, or covering closets are all valid solutions that are part of a trend moving away from minimalism and challenging the concept of "less is more."

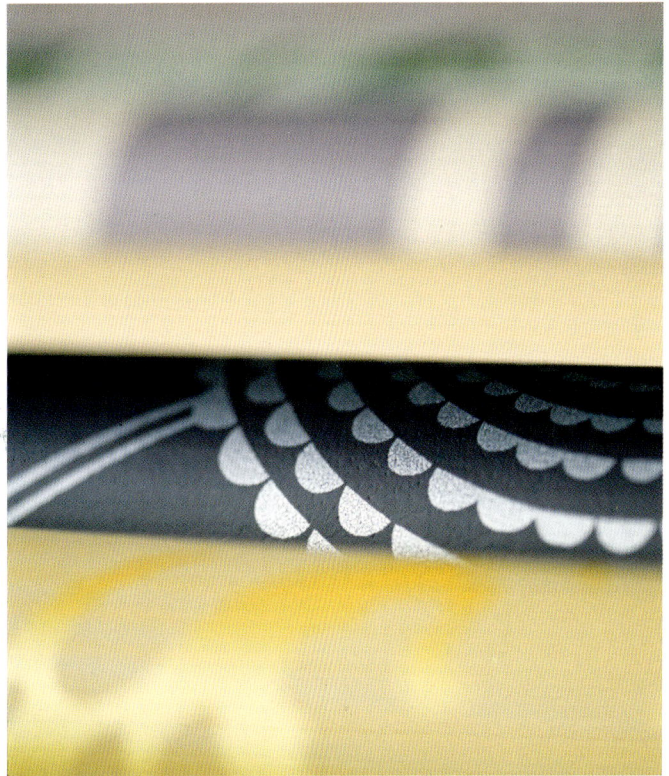

The following practical examples of wallpapers are intended to stimulate readers' imaginations and to help them find the best option for their homes. This selection has therefore been divided into three groups: retro, moderns, and classics. The first shows a style inspired by the aesthetics of the 1960s and 70s. Its showy designs and lively colors do not lend themselves to indifference. The second includes modern designs with a contemporary feel in which a clear Futurist inspiration can be appreciated. The final group presents prints that were characteristic of the first age of wallpaper, with an abundance of classic themes and motifs to decorate warm and welcoming environments.

# Retro

Within the broad spectrum of designs offered by wallpapers, those inspired by the aesthetics of the 1960s and 70s deserve a special mention.

These designs began to appear in fashionable cafés and pubs, and stood out for their colors and forms—circles, lines, flowers, and other geometric motifs—clearly influenced by the liberal currents of the moment. These days, the designs are available to everyone to have in their living rooms, dining rooms or bedrooms—even in corners where we would not have imagined they could be so effective.

In this section, a large quantity of sophisticated prints are shown that can easily be combined with both furniture and other decorative elements; at the same time, they can be alternated with walls painted in a wide variety of tones. The practical examples of wallpapers hung in the various rooms shown in the pages that follow are intended to stimulate readers' imaginations and help them to find the best options for their own needs.

The company Tres Tintas BCN was created in 2004 with a commitment to renovate the design of wallpaper and give it a fresh, youthful, and contemporary air. No company is better placed when it comes to this task, since it forms the second generation of Papeles Pintados Aribau (1961). The visiting card of Tres Tintas BCN is the Revival collection, which revitalizes the aesthetics of Pop Art and the spirit of the 1970s. Wallpaper series based on geometric motifs with a striking chromatic range take us to the golden age of wallpaper in Europe. The reissuing of these designs was welcomed with an enthusiasm that was reflected in both the specialist press for the decoration sector and the supplements of the most important newspapers, confirming that wallpaper had awakened from its lethargy and was once more in the forefront of decorative fashion products.

LINES

HEXAGON ▶

SQUARE

RETRO

RETRO

POPPY

On the following pages:
**ALMOND TREE** | For Jacob Delafon in Casa Decor
Architects: Meritxell Cuartero and Paula Olabarría

RETRO

# VERUSO

The 1970s were truly a vibrant time, and those of us old enough to remember the dizzy motifs and colorful designs that inundated the walls of practically every home do so with great affection. Keen not to have this style era consigned to history, Veruso has devoted itself exclusively to designing prints inspired by the wallpapers of the 1970s. Indeed, the attractive colors and patterns of these wallpapers regularly come back into fashion and can most often be seen in the homes of young people who have rediscovered this fashion trend.

HIPNOS | For IKEA

BIELEFELD | For IKEA

**SILENUS** | For IKEA

RETRO

ABRAX | For DIESEL

**VERUSO TWO** | For Designdowntown NY

**DAGON** | For DIESEL

VENUS | For IKEA

Pages 42–43: APOLLO

**VERUSO ONE** | For IKEA

VERUSO ILLUSION

# Moderns

The style or tendency of wallpapers in this section is the reflection of contemporary design. In some cases, clear Futurist inspiration can be appreciated, while others tend more toward small works of art printed individually or in sequences.

This group offers the greatest diversity of designs and ideas, since they are the wallpapers that most take advantage of technical advances in digital image processing and the latest digital systems for printing or reproduction in large formats. What's more, there is a massive variety of materials printed on—different thicknesses, different textures, and different finishes from gloss with specific varnishes to embossing that achieves a three-dimensional effect.

In its second collection, Tres Tintas BCN set out to revive eclecticism and encourage a mixture of styles and trends by placing its faith in the talent of five young designers—Enric Jardí, Sophie Leblanc, Izqui, Julieta Álvarez, and Marta Fernández—each coming from a different area of design. These designers have reinterpreted a range of artistic styles in the light of the 21st century, which has fully revisited the characteristics that wallpaper once had. The result is a youthful, innovative, and contemporary collection capable of satisfying the sensibility of modern generations with its diversity of styles and chromatic variety. It is undoubtedly a collection capable of provoking a sense of déjà vu for those who grew up with their bedroom walls decorated with exquisite designs.

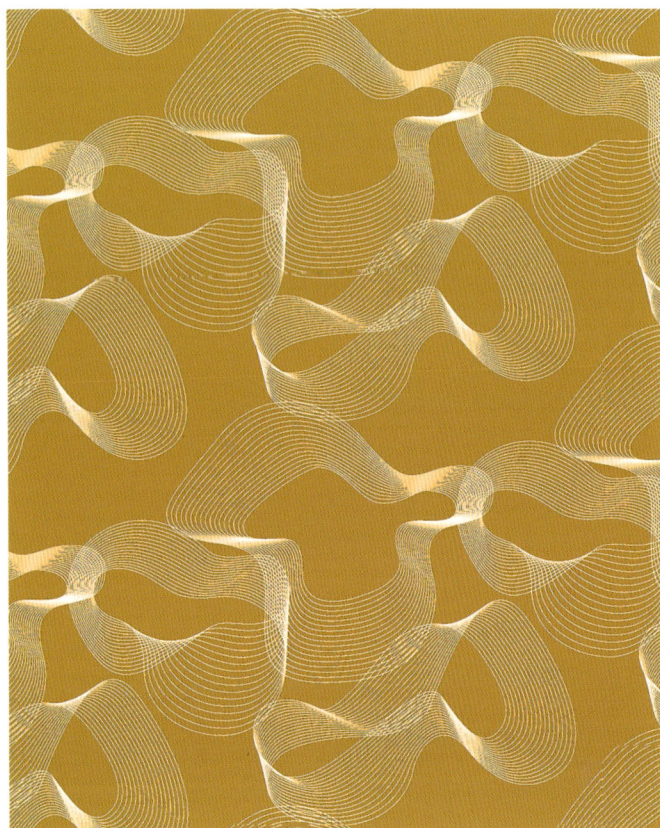

WAVES

TVS

LAMPS

WAVES

IRISES

MODERNS

GALAXIES

MODERNS

BIRDS

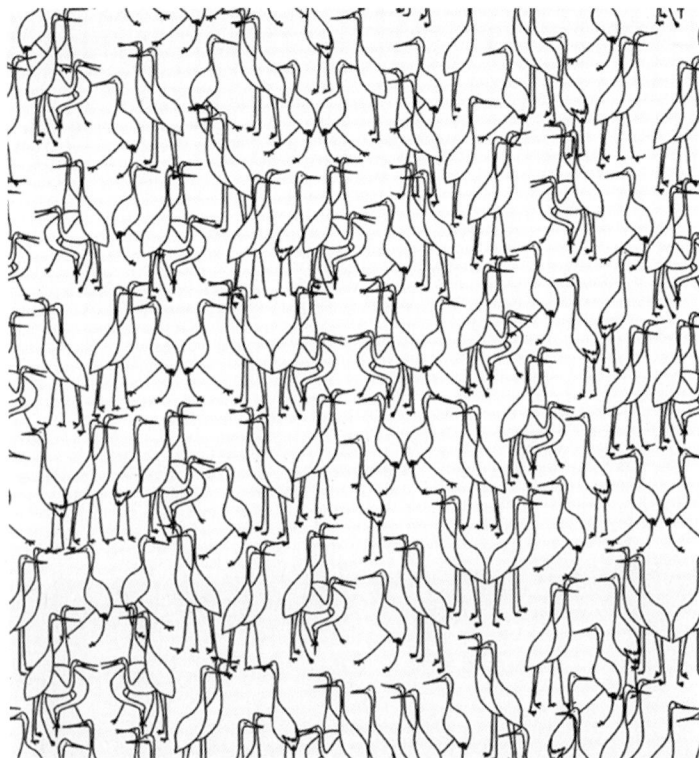

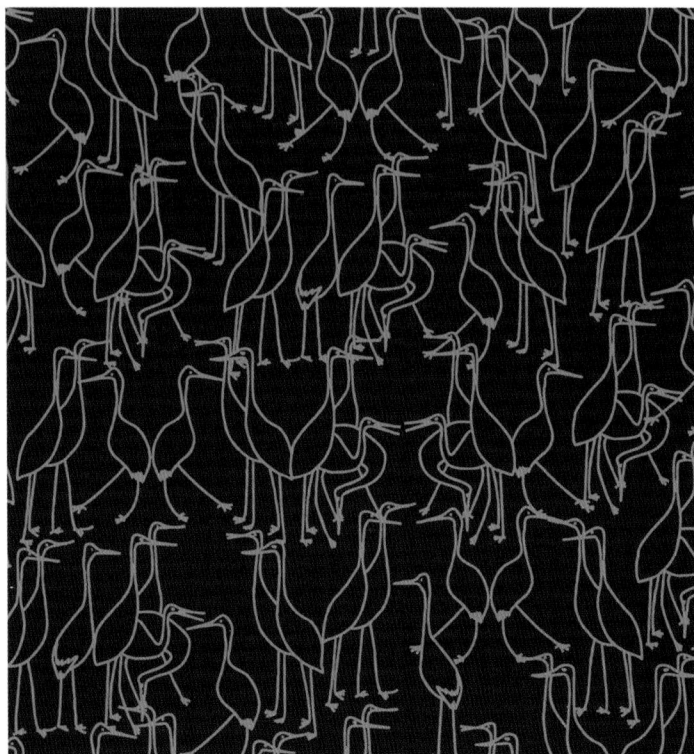

DUCKS

MODERNS

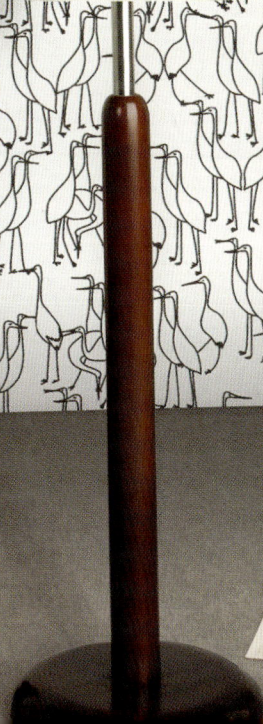

Claude Closky is an emerging artist whose works embrace many facets of Plastic Arts, including the creation of wallpapers. In this field he specializes in a very unusual type of design: he takes decorative motifs that are uncommon and uses them on paper in a decontextualized form. An example of this is a design he has called "Untitled (Nasdaq)," which comprises a mixture of series of numbers, figures, and letters. Based on the same approach, he also uses texts enlarged and in perspective, almost always with black and white. Occasionally, he makes use of color in the backgrounds. Alternatively, he uses tones or duotones on images in four-color print. Close observation of his work reveals enlarged typographic fonts, tribal icons, and even images of contemporary products, which, when extrapolated, produce a series with a retro feel to it.

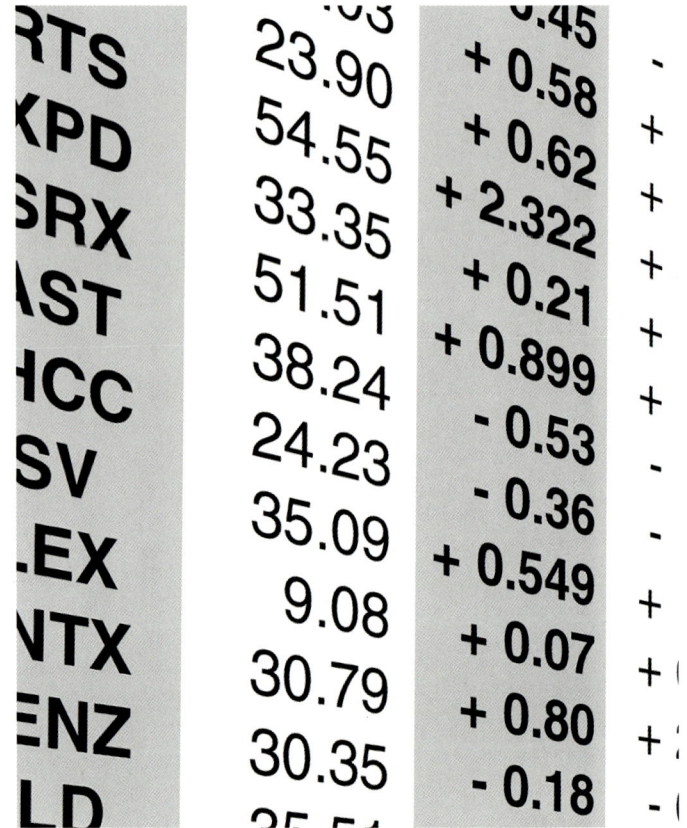

**AUGMENTATION AND REDUCTION** | Interiors by Frédéric Druot for the Pompidou Centre in Paris, France ▶

**UNTITLED (MARABOUT)** | Voilà installation for the Museum of Modern Art in Paris, France

à Nett-mini, Sport-auto, vent glacé, Roche Foucauld, céramique, Galabru, Microsoft, Soft Inter, diplômé, lycéen, Internet, Nett-mini, Géant Vert, [...]

Léant Vert, Look Pressing, Mini, Minitel, Telecom, Hollywood, Woodpecker, méchant look, Look Pressing, Sing Tao, Hollywood, [...]

dans le coup, recyclé, Cléopâtre, patriarche, architecte, Tectona, naphtaline, Line Renaud, Cléopâtre, [...]

recyclé, Cléopâtre, Renault 16, seize soupapes, papa poule, poules farcies, siphonné, Renault 16, seize soupapes, [...]

cine Renaud, nez qui coule, cool Raoul, Oulipo, peau de pêche, pêche au gros, Gromyko, [...]

cies, siphonné, Gromyko, Collargol, Goldorak, raccordé, dés pipés, pélican, cancéreux, rebrousse-poil, [...]

è? pêche au gros, rebrousse-poil, poil aux seins, Saint-Rémy, mis à nu, numéro, Robespierre, [...]

pipés, pélican, cancéreux, Robespierre, Pier Import, Port-Marly, Livret A, allégé, égérie, érigé, génétique, [...]

emy, mis à nu, numéro, ticket chic, chicorée, Réaumur, mur du son, son Dolby, bigoudi, [...]

ivret A, allégé, égérie, érigé, génétique, ticket chic, chicorée, Réaumur, mur du son, son Dolby, [...]

aumur, mur du son, son Dolby, bigoudi, Dynastar, Star Pizza, Pizza 30, 3615, Quinze de France, [...]

zza 30, 3615, Quinze de France, France Culture, Culture Rock, rocking-chair, Tchernobil, Bilbao, [...]

rocking-chair, Tchernobil, Bilbao, Obao, Othello, Lolita, Tahiti, timoré, résolu, [...]

timoré, résolu, lumineux, nœud coulant, lambada, Dagobert, Bergasol, solitaire, terre battue, [...]

ergasol, solitaire, terre battue, tu l'as dit, dix mille balles, balle perdue, du gâteau, taux d'urée, [...]

erdue, du gâteau, taux d'urée, rhéostat, Stabilo, Loto 7, 7 sur 7, c'est écrit, cri du cœur, [...]

c'est écrit, cri du cœur, cœur battant, temps à perdre, perdre la tête, tête d'affiche, fiche [...]

tête, tête d'affiche, fiche tricot, cocaïne, Inch'Allah, à la une, Uniprix, prix sympas, [...]

rix, prix sympas, Pamela, la bohème, MK2, K2R, RDA, DAT, TVA, AFP, PEA, A + B, BEP, PER, [...]

AFP, PEA, A + B, BEP, PER, RTL, LCD, DAP, PEL, LSD, DHL, HLM, MCM, MJC, CDD, DST, [...]

HLM, MCM, MJC, CDD, DST, TVE, EPS, SFR, RMI, IUT, UTA, AOM, MBK, KOH, HIV, VRP, PSU, [...]

AOM, MBK, KOH, HIV, VRP, PSU, USA, AZT, THX, XTC, CRS, SFP, PG, PAO, OPA, ABC, CAP, PSG, GSM, [...]

PAO, OPA, ABC, CAP, PSG, GSM, MST, THX, XTC, CRS, SFP, PNB, BDV, VHS, SPA, AEG, GPL, [...]

PVC, CRS, SFP, PNB, BDV, VHS, SPA, AEG, GPL, LCI, RN, NRJ, [...]

RJ, IPS, SDF, FMR, RER, RPR, RAS, SAS, SOS, ONU, SW, [...]

MU, UAP, APC, PCC, CCC, CCA, ACC, CCI, GIC, CEE, PPP, PTT, [...]

AT, TTC, CCA, ACC, CCI, GIC, CEE, FRI, [...]

RJ, IPS, SDF, FMR, [...]

BS, EVA, ADN, NRS, [...]

**AUGMENTATION AND REDUCTION** | Interiors by Frédéric Druot for the Pompidou Centre in Paris, France

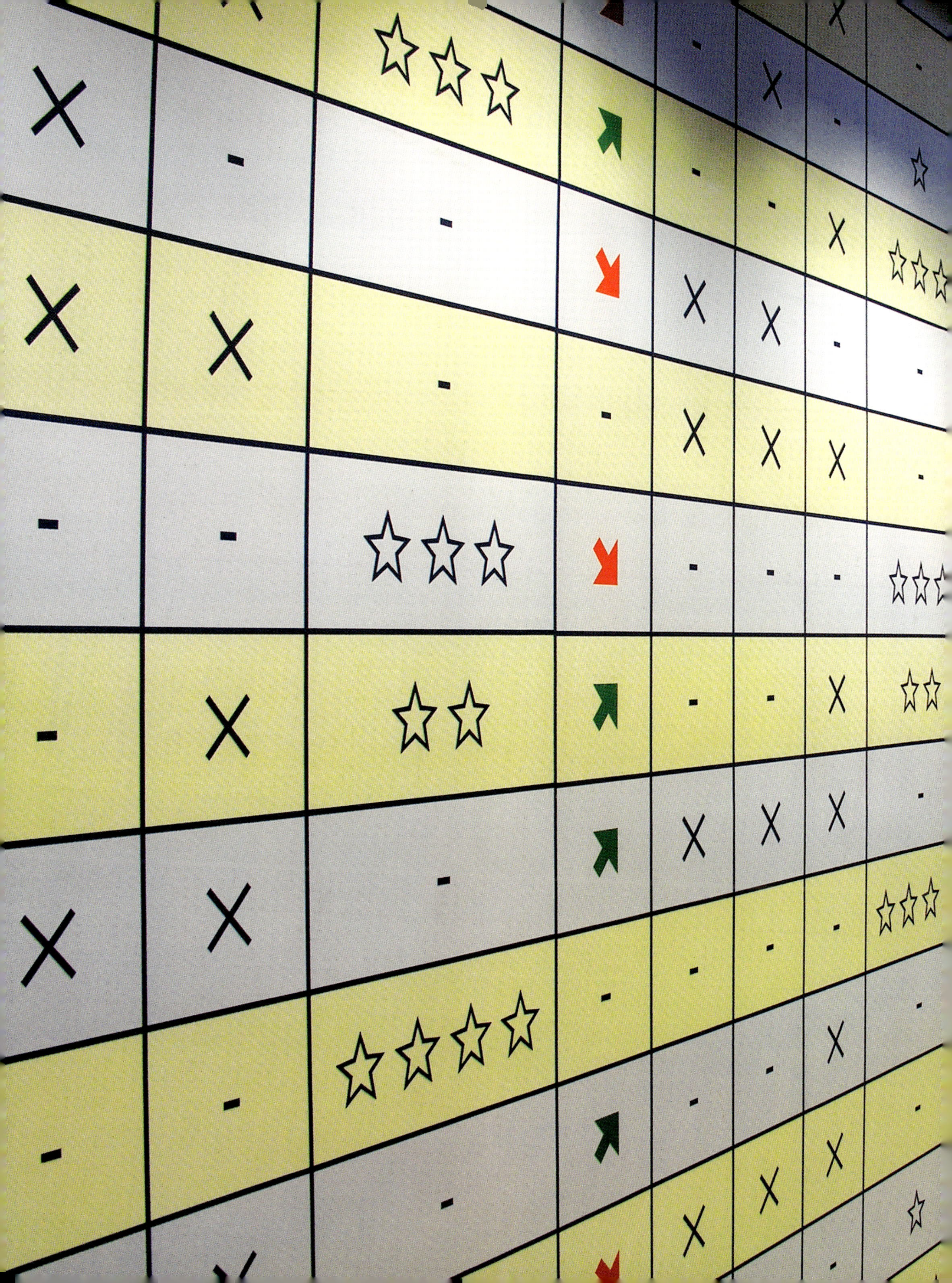

HIPNOS | Veruso

UNTITLED (TATTOOS) | Installation at the Cartier Foundation in Paris, France ▶

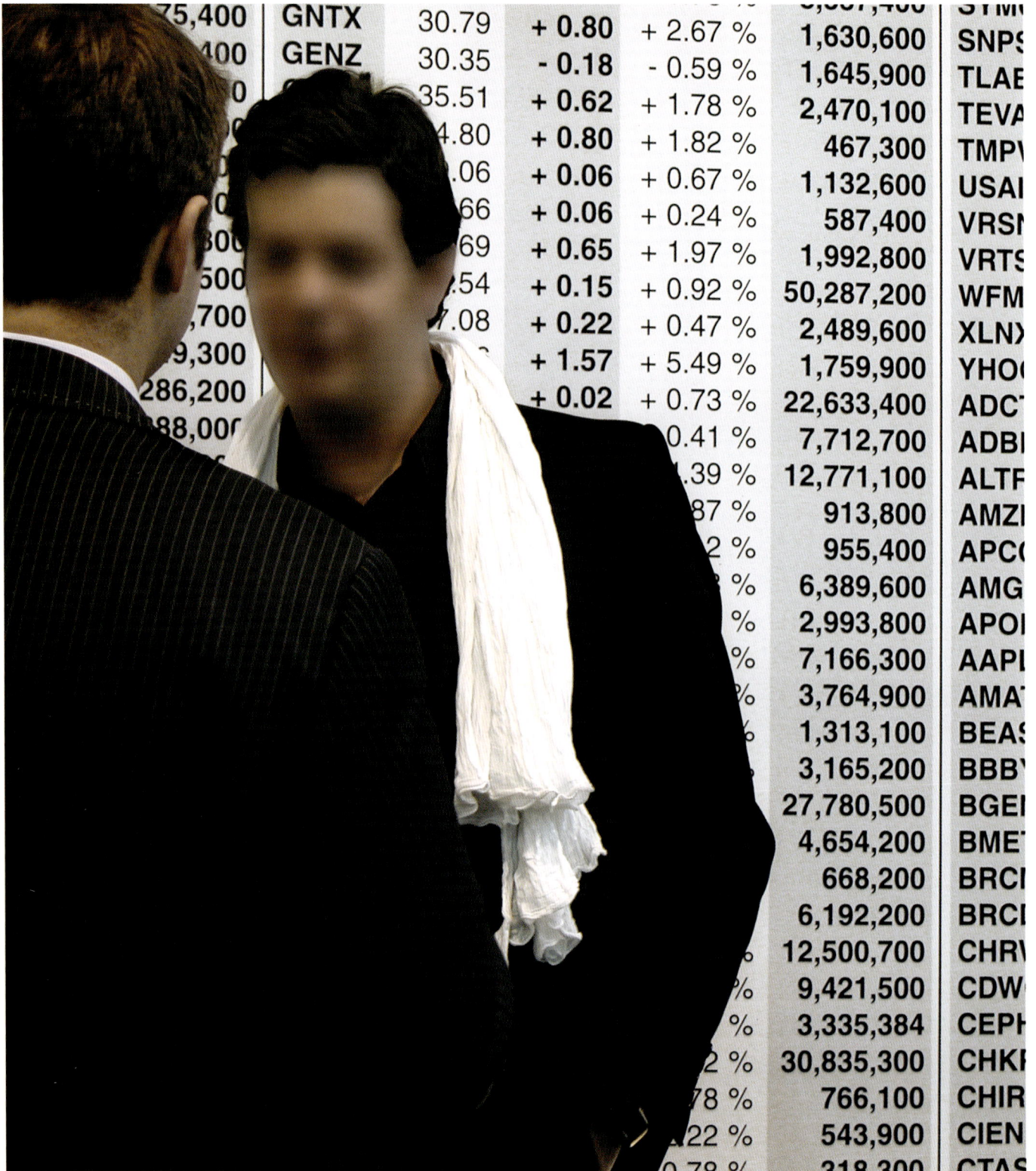

**UNTITLED (NASDAQ)** | Installation in Mudam, Luxembourg

Stock quotation table (columns partially cropped at left and right edges).

| Last | Chg | Chg % | Volume |
|---|---|---|---|
| .93 | + 0.45 | − 0.48 % | ,368,000 |
| .90 | + 0.58 | − 1.75 % | 16,794,000 |
| .55 | + 0.62 | + 0.84 % | 728,700 |
| .35 | + 2.322 | + 2.66 % | 1,729,800 |
| .51 | + 0.21 | + 4.45 % | 5,098,100 |
| .24 | + 0.899 | + 0.63 % | 4,356,400 |
| .23 | − 0.53 | + 1.78 % | 7,340,100 |
| .09 | − 0.36 | − 1.37 % | 524,400 |
| .08 | + 0.549 | − 1.46 % | 1,239,200 |
| .79 | + 0.07 | + 1.59 % | 1,288,800 |
| .35 | + 0.80 | + 0.78 % | 900,100 |
| .51 | − 0.18 | + 2.67 % | 1,639,000 |
| .80 | + 0.62 | − 0.59 % | 8,337,400 |
| .06 | + 0.80 | + 1.78 % | 1,630,600 |
| .66 | + 0.06 | + 1.82 % | 1,645,900 |
| .69 | + 0.06 | + 0.67 % | 2,470,100 |
| .54 | + 0.65 | + 0.24 % | 467,300 |
| .08 | + 0.15 | + 1.97 % | 1,132,600 |
| .16 | + 0.22 | + 0.92 % | 587,400 |
| .77 | + 1.57 | + 0.47 % | 1,992,800 |
| .39 | + 0.02 | + 5.49 % | 50,287,200 |
| | + 0.03 | + 0.73 % | 2,489,600 |
| | + 1.64 | + 0.41 % | 1,759,900 |
| | | + 4.39 % | 22,633,400 |
| | | | 7,712,700 |
| | | | 12,771,100 |
| | | | 913,800 |

| Symbol | Last | Chg | Chg % | Vol |
|---|---|---|---|---|
| M | 19.00 | + 0.11 | − 0.61 % | 543 |
| PIXR | 18.01 | + 0.29 | + 0.38 % | 318 |
| QLGC | 56.18 | + 0.03 | + 1.55 % | 1,504 |
| QCOM | 37.77 | − 0.74 | + 0.17 % | 1,809 |
| RFMD | 35.7 | + 1.37 | − 1.30 % | 5,052 |
| ROST | 8.10 | + 1.44 | + 3.76 % | 1,304 |
| RYAAY | 42.85 | − 0.01 | + 4.20 % | 429 |
| SANM | 42.39 | + 0.38 | − 0.12 % | 10,722 |
| SEBL | 4.21 | + 2.29 | + 0.89 % | 16,144 |
| SIAL | 8.00 | + 0.30 | + 5.71 % | 940 |
| SSCC | 49.1 | + 0.05 | + 7.67 % | 450 |
| SPLS | 16.02 | + 0.25 | + 0.63 % | 6,957 |
| SBUX | 17.93 | + 0.122 | + 0.51 % | 8,161 |
| SUNW | 21.12 | + 0.46 | + 0.77 % | 479 |
| SYMC | 3.55 | − 0.08 | + 2.63 % | 1,437 |
| SNPS | 43.85 | + 0.17 | − 0.38 % | 2,929 |
| TLAB | 42.25 | + 1.17 | + 5.03 % | 3,934 |
| TEVA | 8.27 | − 4.67 | + 2.74 % | 53,416 |
| TMPW | 39.09 | + 0.22 | − 9.95 % | 3,621 |
| USAI | 12.12 | − 0.19 | + 2.73 % | 10,175 |
| VRSN | 24.22 | + 0.081 | − 0.48 % | 3,335 |
| VRTS | 8.55 | − 0.09 | + 0.67 % | 2,356 |
| WFMI | 17.03 | + 0.062 | − 0.37 % | 801 |
| XLNX | 53.88 | + 0.08 | + 0.73 % | 2,194 |
| YHOO | 22.94 | − 0.06 | − 0.11 % | 3,148 |
| ADCT | 18.10 | + 0.91 | + 0.47 % | 4,059 |
| ADBE | 2.65 | + 0.50 | + 4.13 % | 533 |
| ALTR | 26.30 | + 0.35 | + 2.84 % | 10,172 |
| AMZN | 13.38 | + 0.70 | + 15.22 % | 14,286 |
| APCC | 20.52 | + 0.13 | + 2.73 % | 2,888 |
| | 16.42 | + 0.95 | + 0.98 % | 11,858 |
| | | + 0.37 | + 4.85 % | 8,777 |
| | | − 0.13 | + 2.31 % | 1,979 |
| | | | − 0.26 % | 8,294 |
| | | | | 1,617 |

**UNTITLED (SUPERMARKET)** | Installation in the Espace Royal Monterey of the Banque Générale de Luxembourg

The Tapeten Agentur company sees wallpaper as an essential element that can alter an individual's well-being. It considers that, since wallpaper can occupy the largest surfaces that exist in the home—the walls—it is necessary to select carefully those prints that will best respond to each person's emotional needs. It claims that all the wallpapers in its Gohome line—which includes the Octopus, Caviar, and Lobster designs—create unique stories and cannot be compared to any other designs on the market. Its creations are exclusive, inspired by its own ideas and produced by hand. It combines modern digital technology in printing with innovative materials and technical traditions—achieving surprising results.

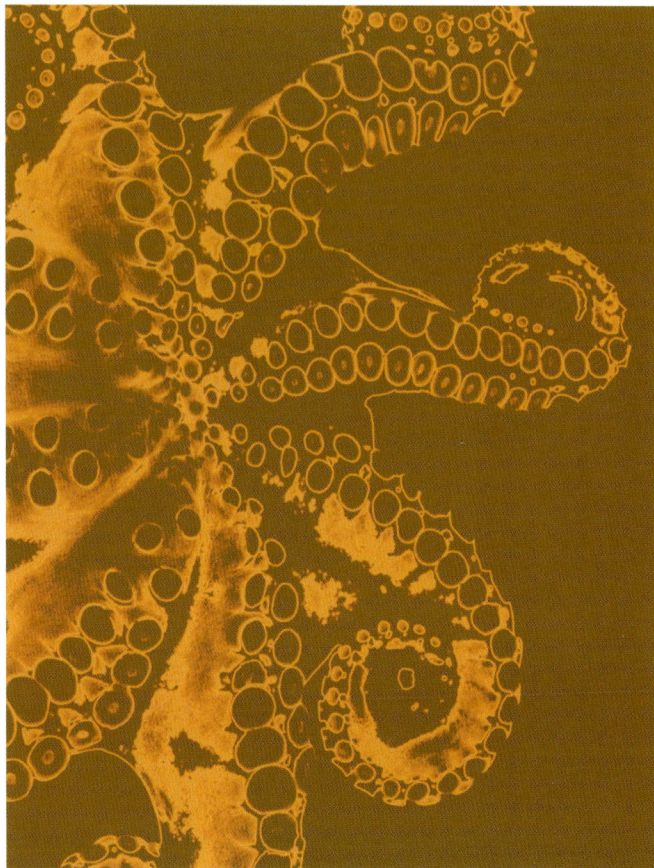

OCTOPUS

CAVIAR

CAVIAR

LOBSTER

Pages 82–83: OCTOPUS ▶

MODERNS

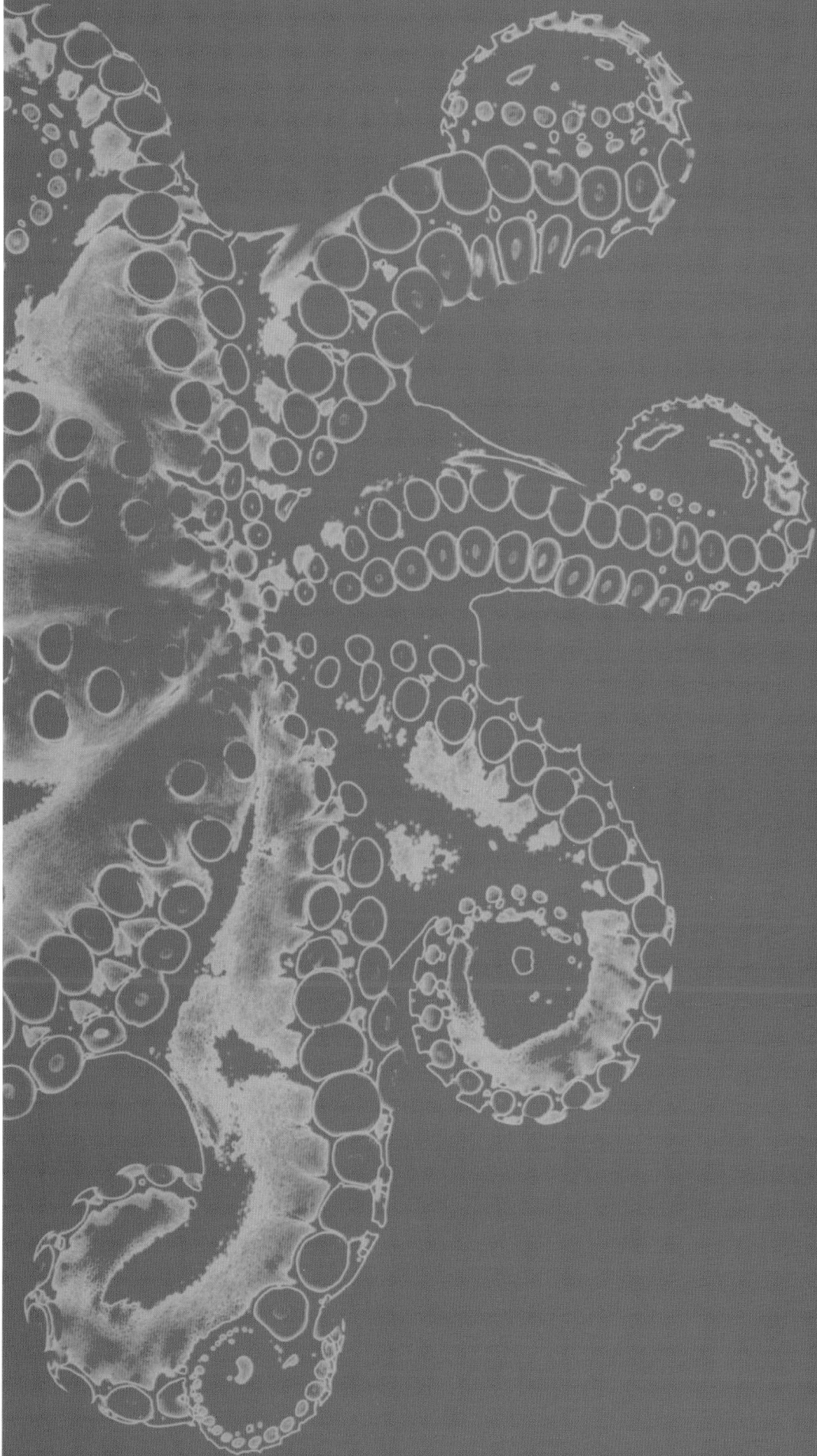

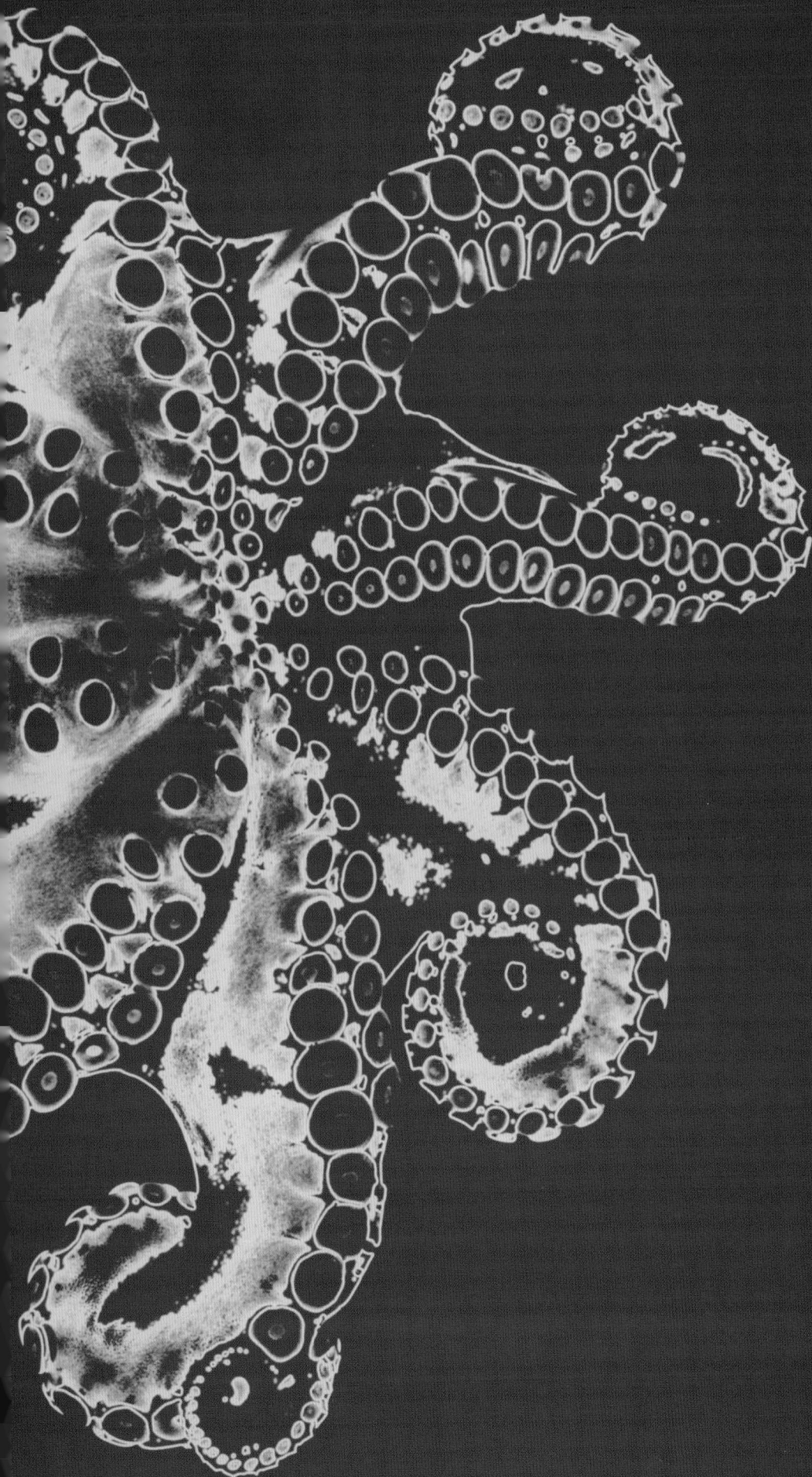

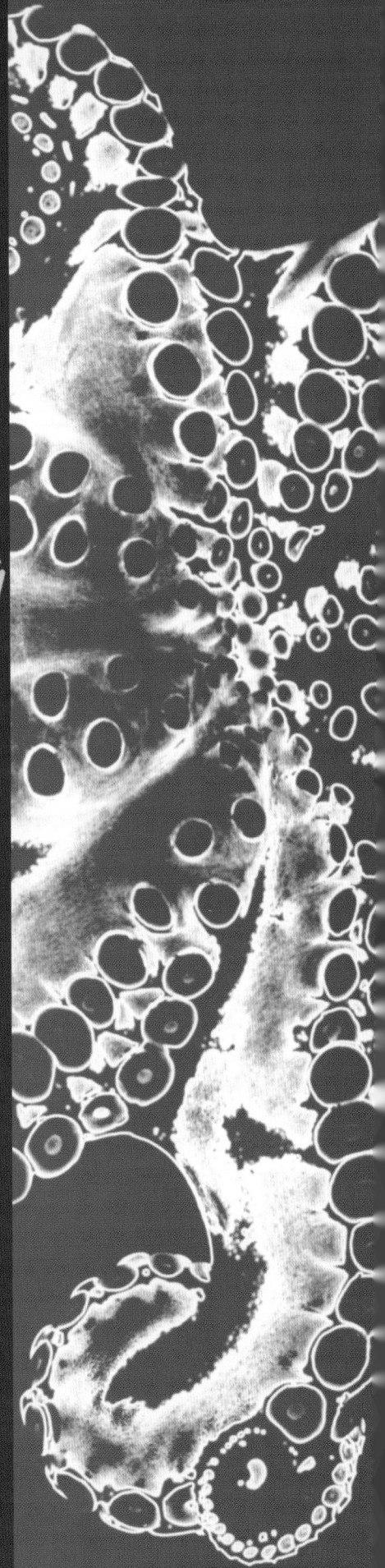

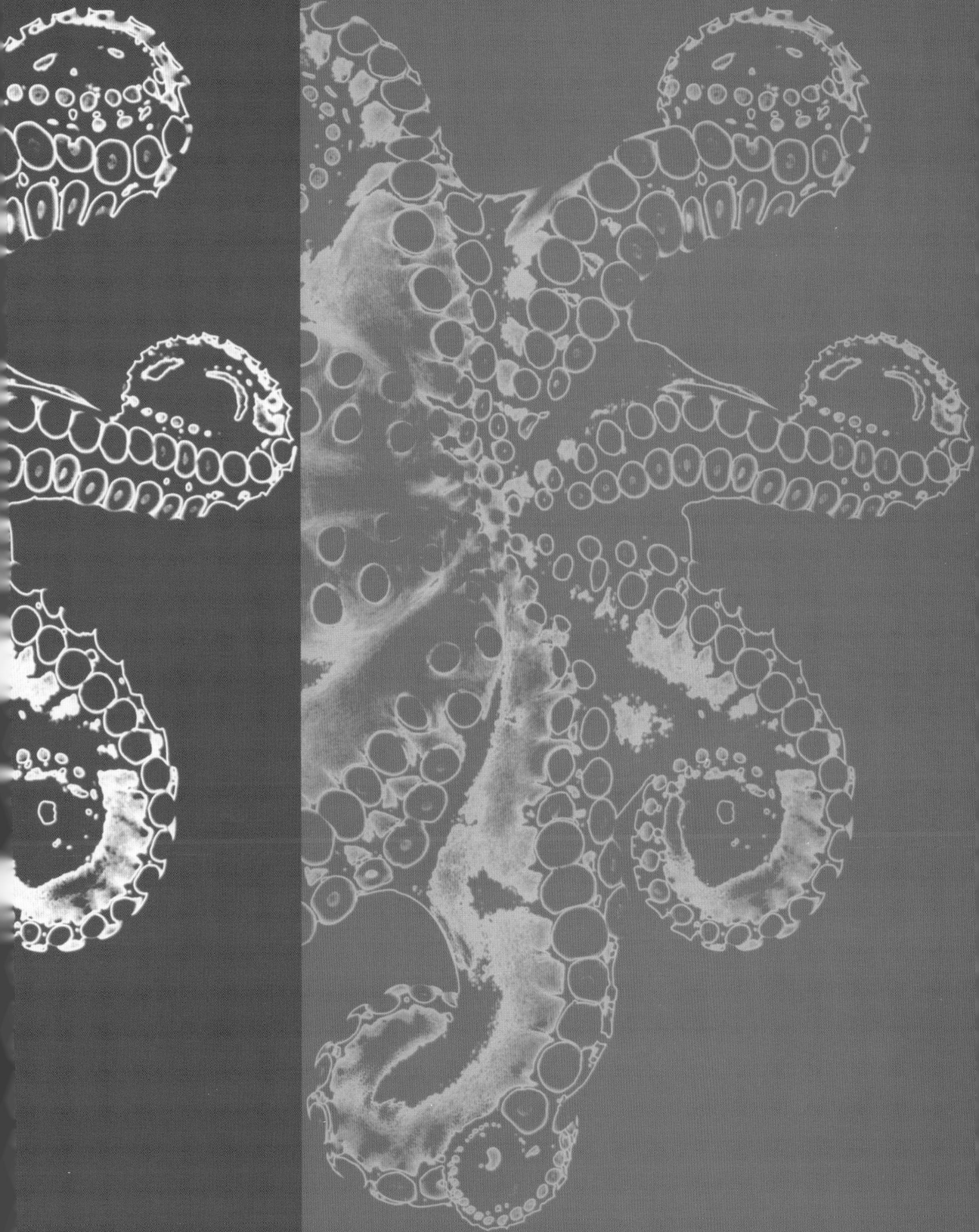

Interior designer Erica Wakerly produces her own wallpapers with designs inspired by organic and graphic elements. In her work she combines new techniques and materials with a human component—for example, a hand-made pattern with a digital print. Her results are modern, but not exclusively for interiors that follow the latest trends. When installed on the wall, the silver lines in her Angles pattern become very ethereal, capable of interacting with the light and colors of the whole room. The Spiral pattern, on the other hand, works well in small spaces when it is hung vertically, although hung horizontally it also provides a charming dynamic for any environment. Both models have a curious relationship with the space, because they interact with the three dimensions, using an interplay of perspectives to configure the decorative element in question.

ANGLES

SPIRAL

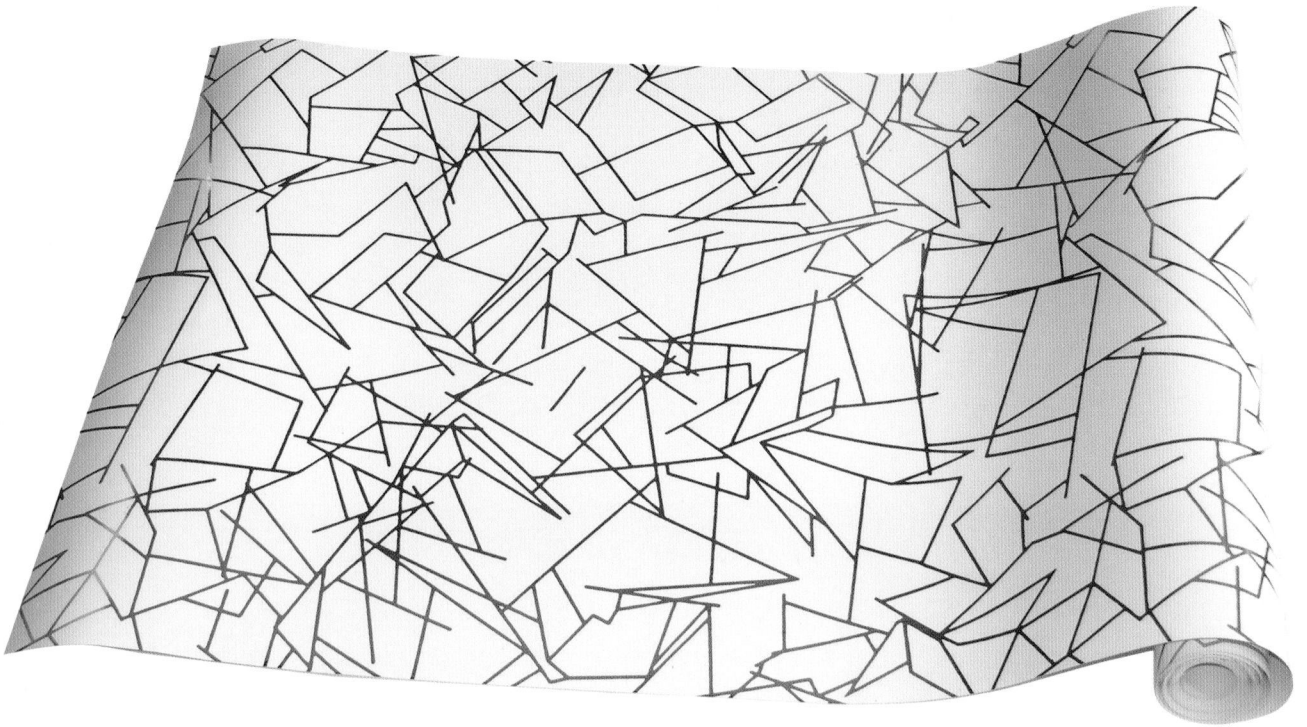

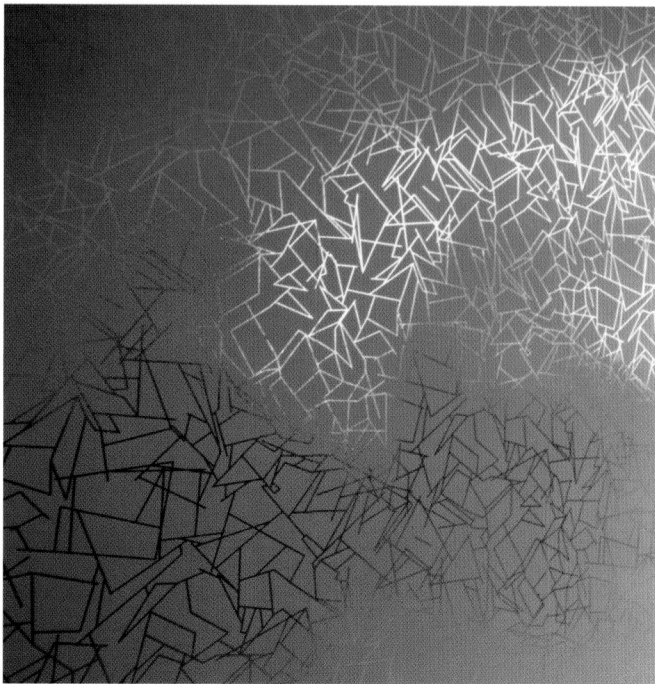

ANGLES

MODERNS

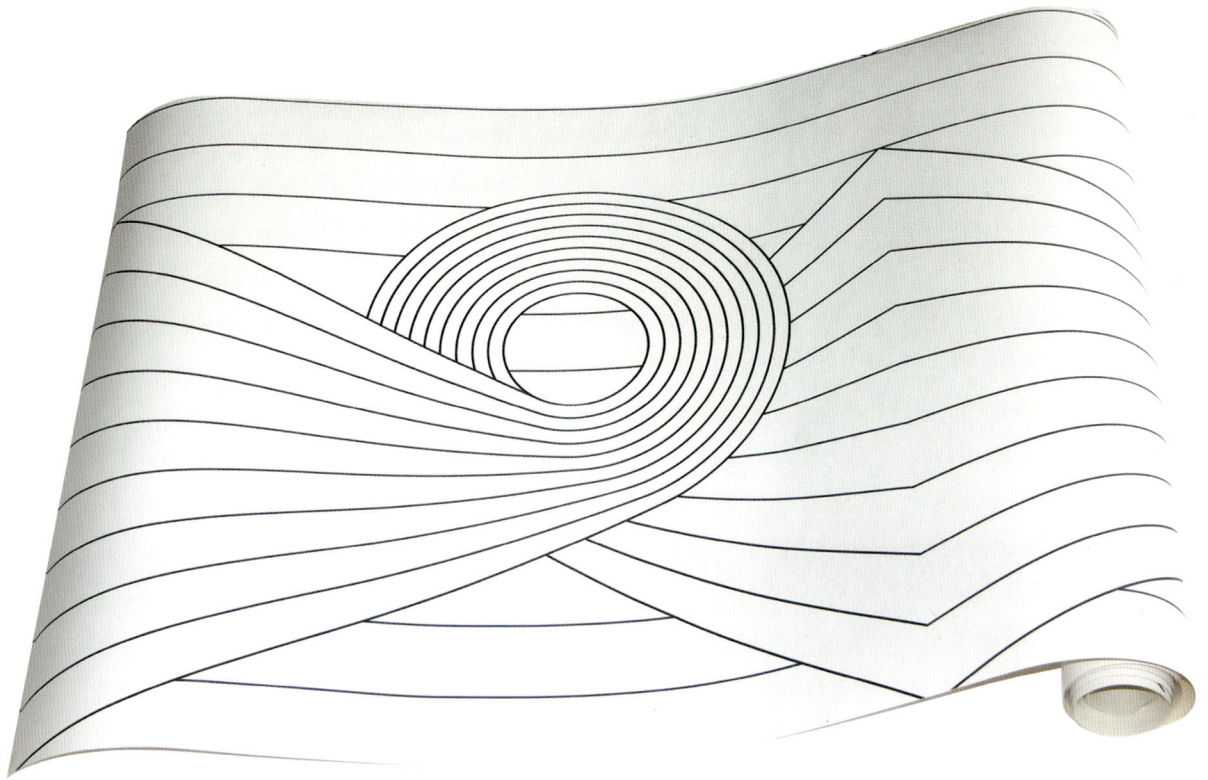

SPIRAL

MODERNS

Habitat was created in the United Kingdom in 1964. Since then, the company has continued to revolutionize the world of home decoration and the industry as a whole through its great innovative spirit. Now, from the hand of Tom Dixon—appointed head of design in 1998—this firm has brought out a collection baptized Very Important Products onto the market, including a series of wallpapers designed by specially invited artists. Orla Kiely, Eley Kishimoto, Matthew Williamson, Roland Mouret, and Barbara Hulanicki are included among those who have participated in this interesting idea and worked on a product that offers the user high-quality designs. Each finds inspiration in different themes—from Art Nouveau to retro style—and all use pastel colors to give them life. The result is a well-conceived series with strong personality and quality.

WILLIAMSON

KISHIMOTO

KIELY ▶

HULANICKI

MODERNS

Johanna Basford's wallpapers are all hand-made in her small studio in Scotland. The source of this brilliant designer's inspiration is the nature surrounding her work base, from where she obtains botanical specimens and even imaginary bugs. She is not a supporter of the production line, so each of her products is printed individually with special inks to achieve pieces rich in detail and pleasant to the touch. The interplay of whites and blacks is prevalent in most of her prints, but all her wallpapers can be acquired in a large variety of colors and finishes—for example, with pearl or bright gloss effect. Basford also creates her prints on cloth, which means customers are able to decorate their rooms with other complementary elements such as drapes or cushions.

CRAZY BOTANIC

INSECTIANA 1

CRAZY BOTANIC

PEKING

MODERNS

# MARKUS BENESCH

Markus Benesch conceived the decorative lines Colorflage and Strip'n Tease in order to offer a useful tool to create an original and novel style to any type of space. As well as wallpaper, the lines include cloth, polyethylene foam furniture, lamps, and paint. The Benesch decorative proposal involves using the same motif both on the walls and in other elements that furnish the room. The result is that furniture almost goes unnoticed, aided by the three-dimensional effects giving rise to striking forms and colors. In short, the space is camouflaged under a uniformity of sensations. The prints focus on a three-dimensional interplay, and use different graphic effects to distort the space and produce optical illusions. Furthermore, customers can decide on the frequency of both the print design and the color that most suits them.

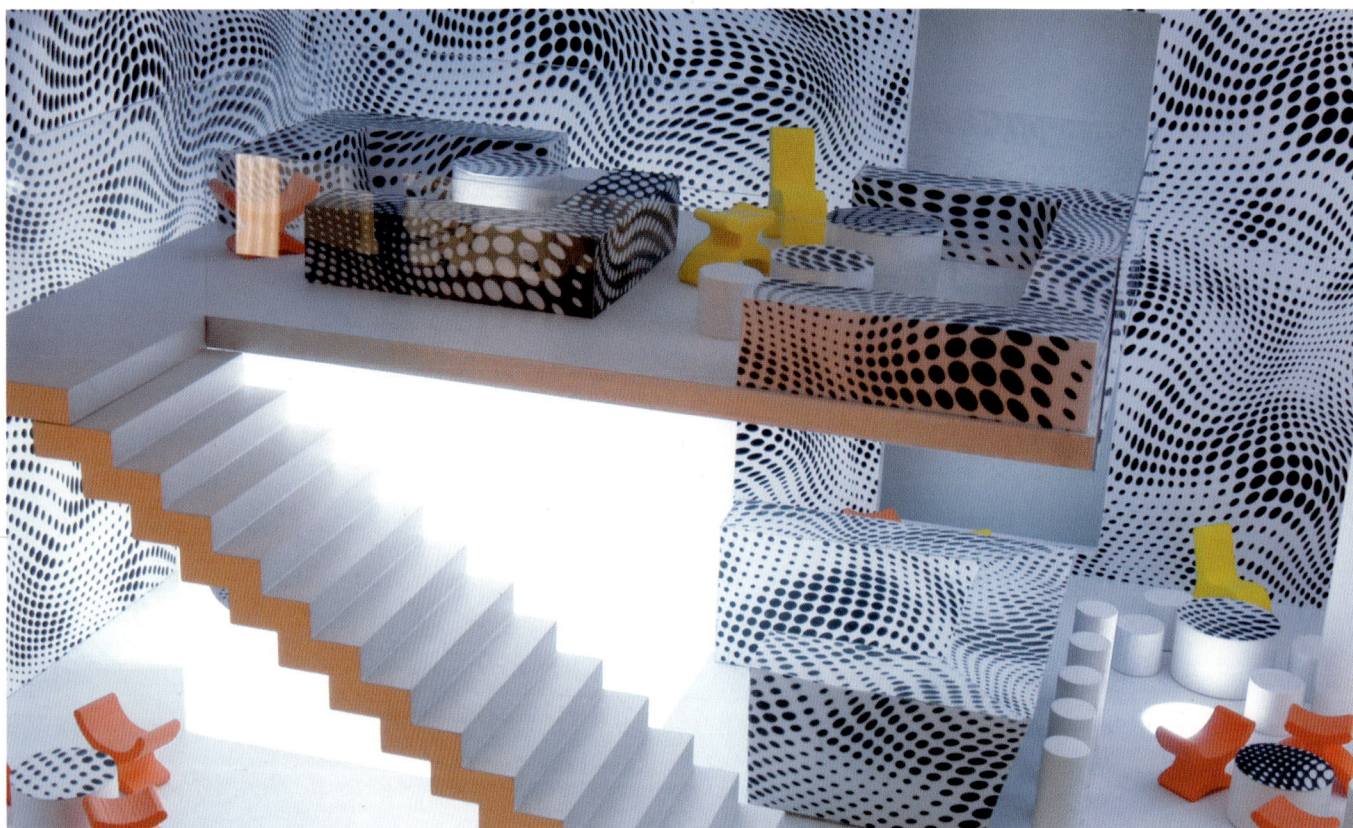

FLOW-DOT

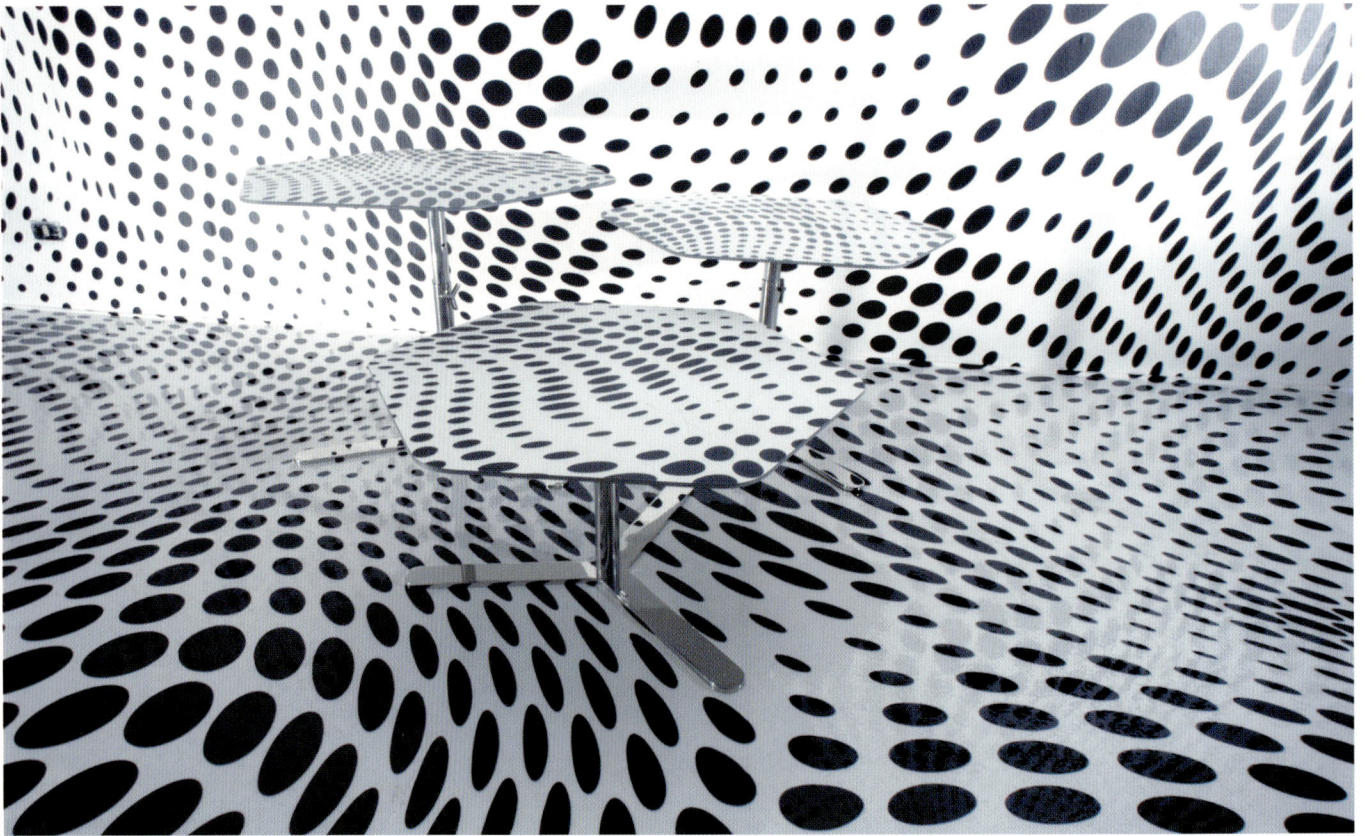

HONEY TABLES

PORTAFORTUNA ARMCHAIR

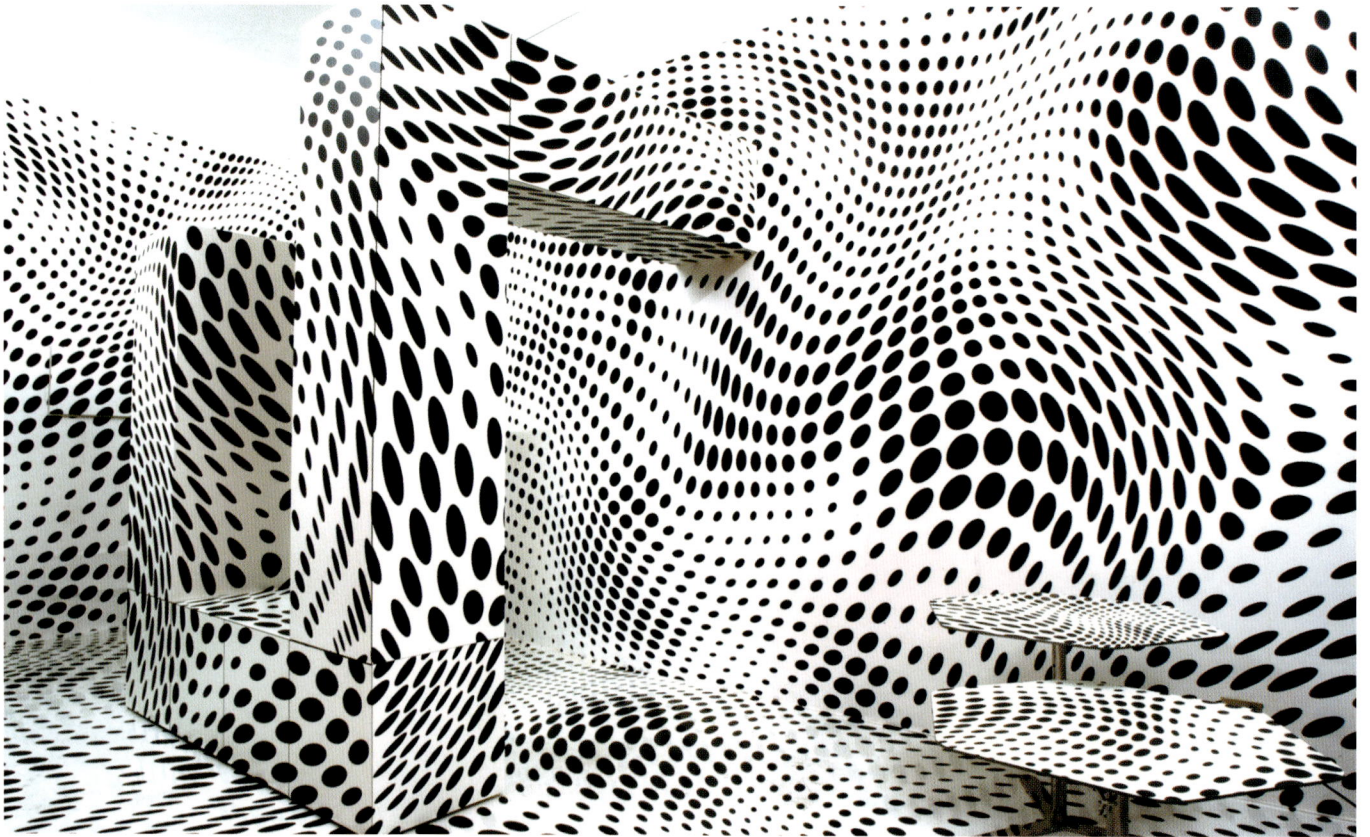
HONEY TABLES

TOCAFORTUNA STOOL

HONEY FOOMY FOAM STOOL ▶

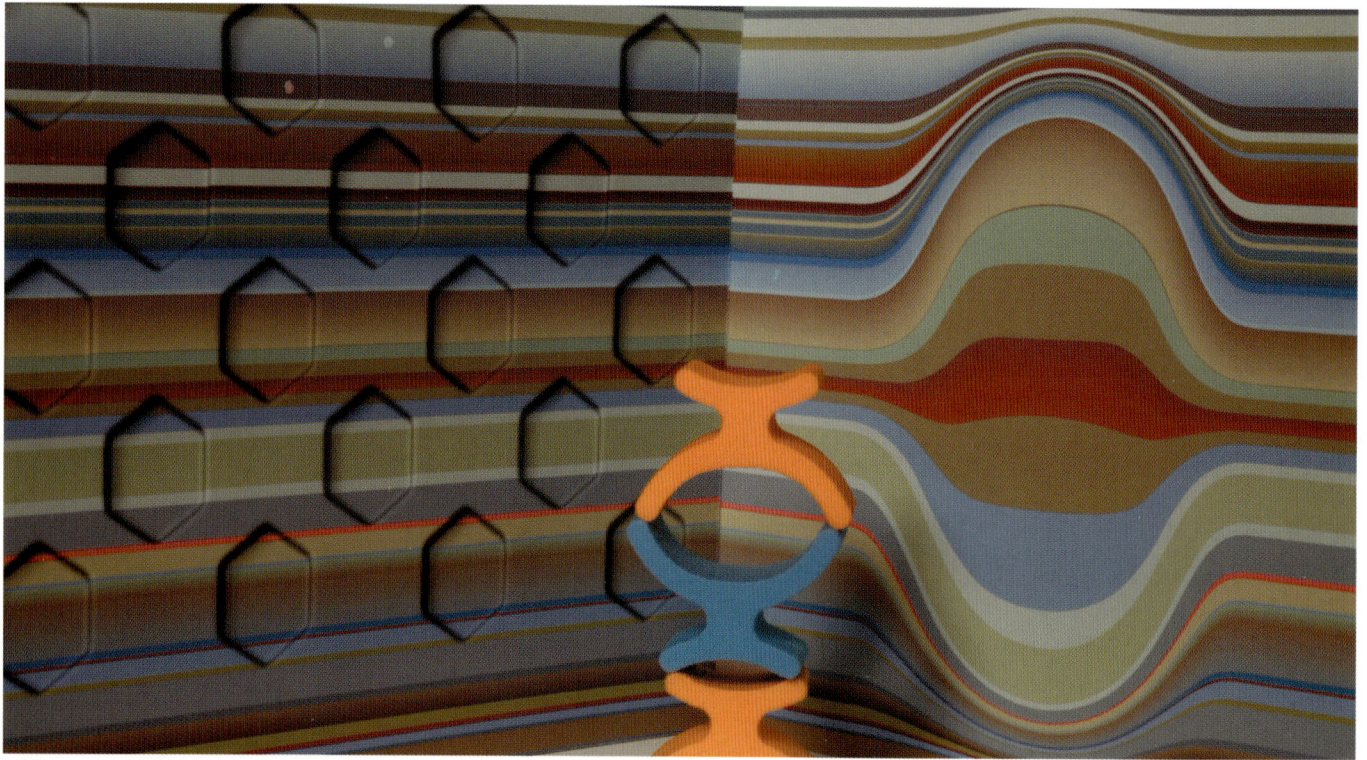

LIPS

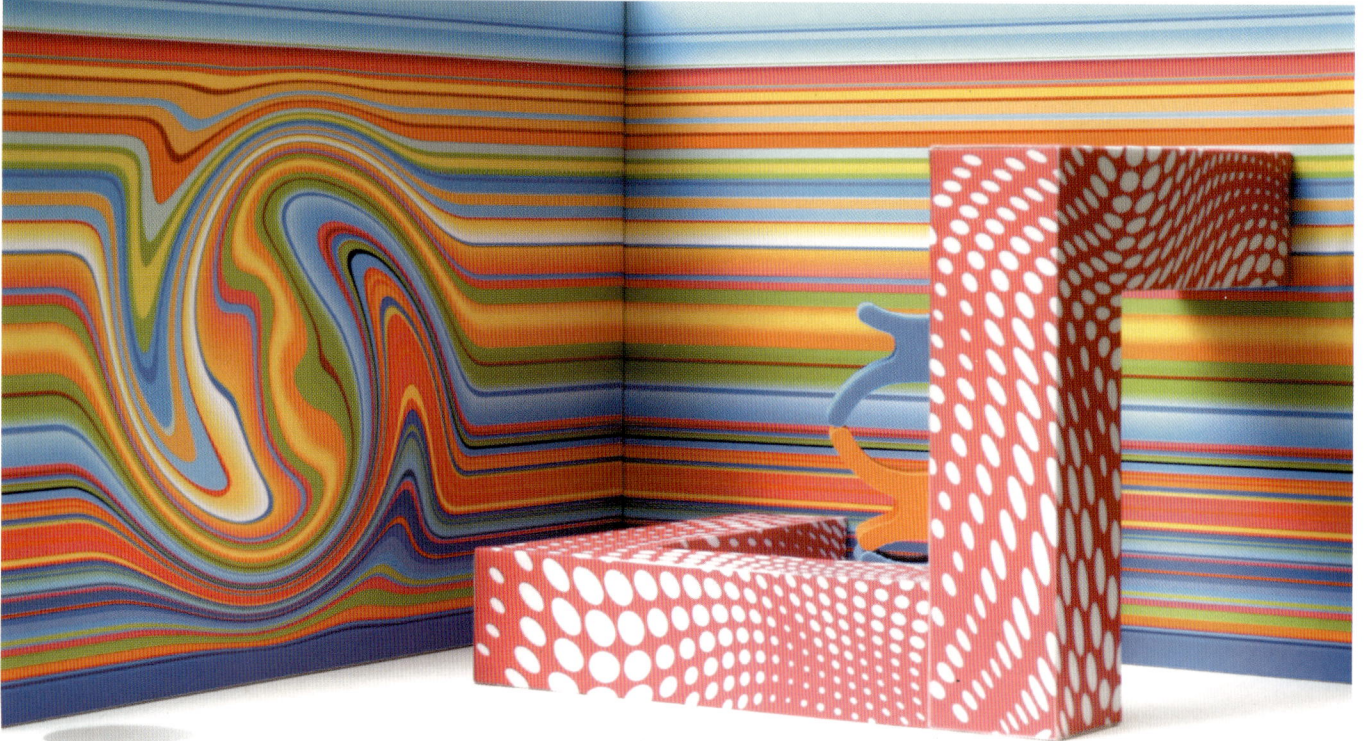

MULTI TWIST

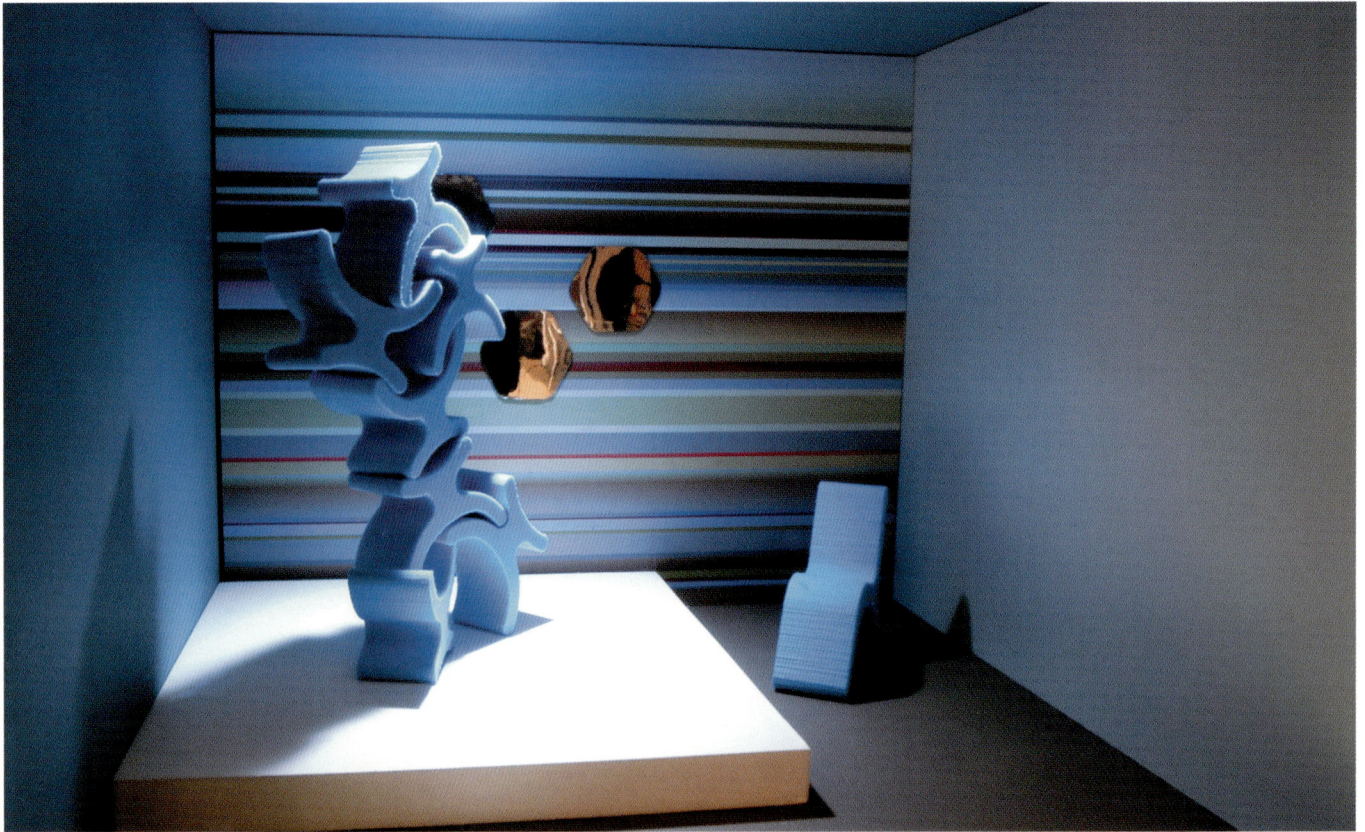

STRIPES

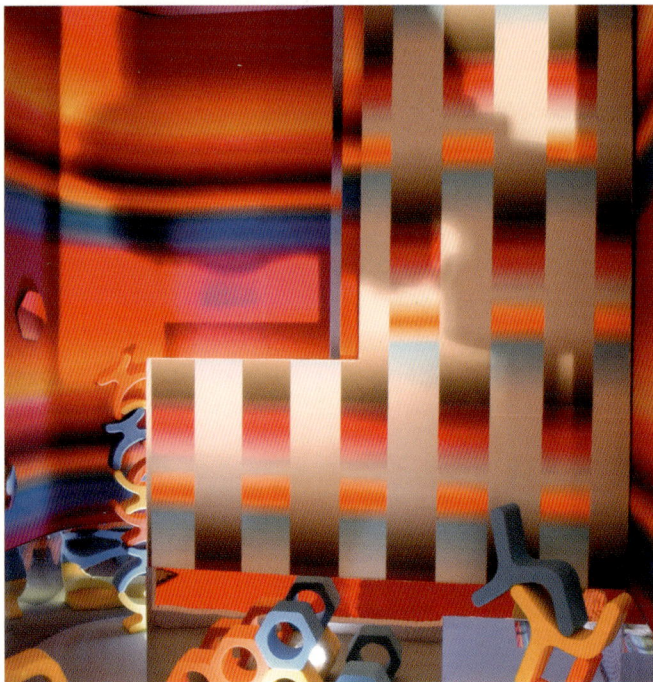

SKY

MODERNS

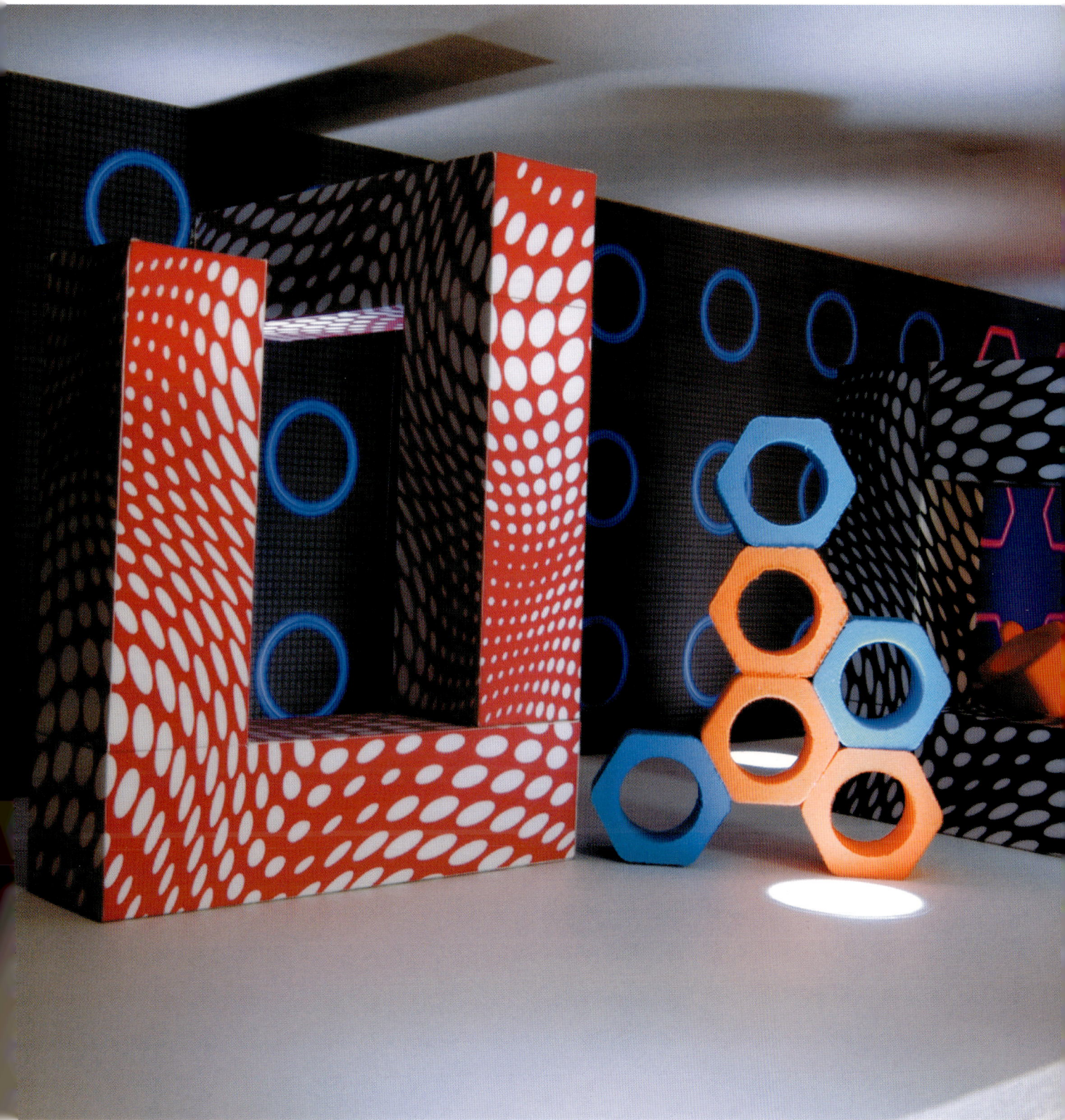

# KUBOAA

With its slogan "Making beautiful papers," Kuboaa is proud to present its latest line of wallpapers for the home, comprising the Sofine collection—full of originality—and another designed jointly with Siecle Colours, for which the palette of colors is the fundamental element. As was already the case in the first collections, all the designs in this new line have been created by Andrew Hardiman, who has achieved considerable critical acclaim and has been named the UK's Young Designer of the Year by the *Telegraph* newspaper. His new designs continue to express an exciting and fresh note, and continue to receive praise in specialist publications such as *Elle Decoration*. Indeed, this magazine promotes the Wallpaper of the Year competition, in the 2005 edition of which Kuboaa was a finalist with its Wistaria design.

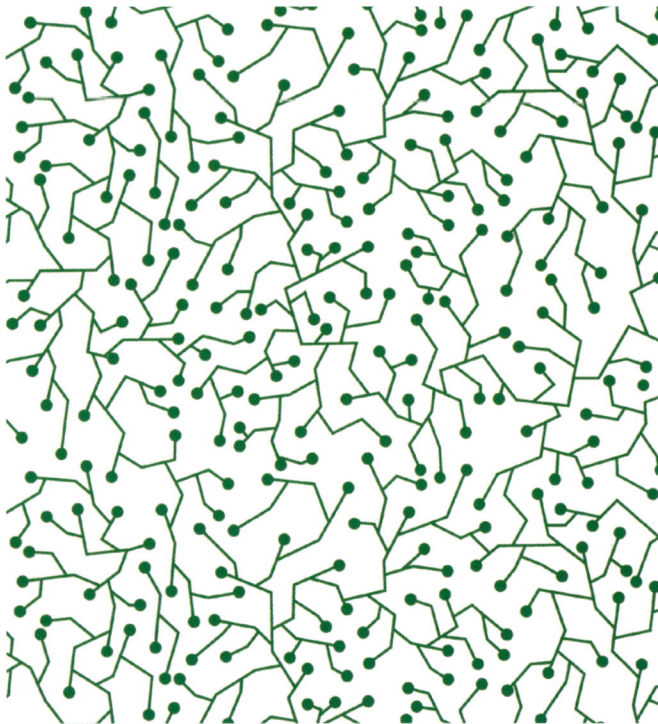

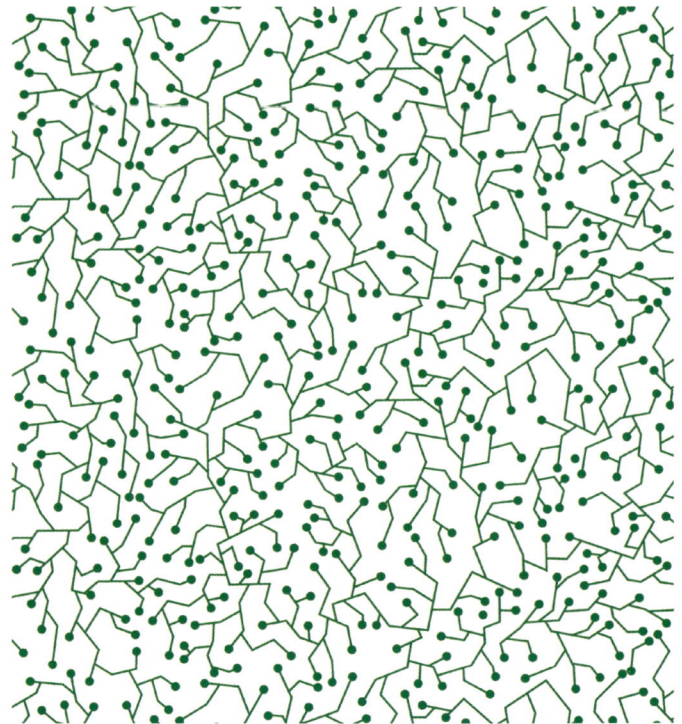

ALLUMETTE | Kuboaa collection with Siecle Colours

WISTARIA ▶

**LUBIEN DAMASK** | Sofine collection

**WISTARIA** | Kuboaa collection with Siecle Colours

**ESCALATING MAN** | Kuboaa collection with Siecle Colours

**REGAL SQUARE** | Sofine collection

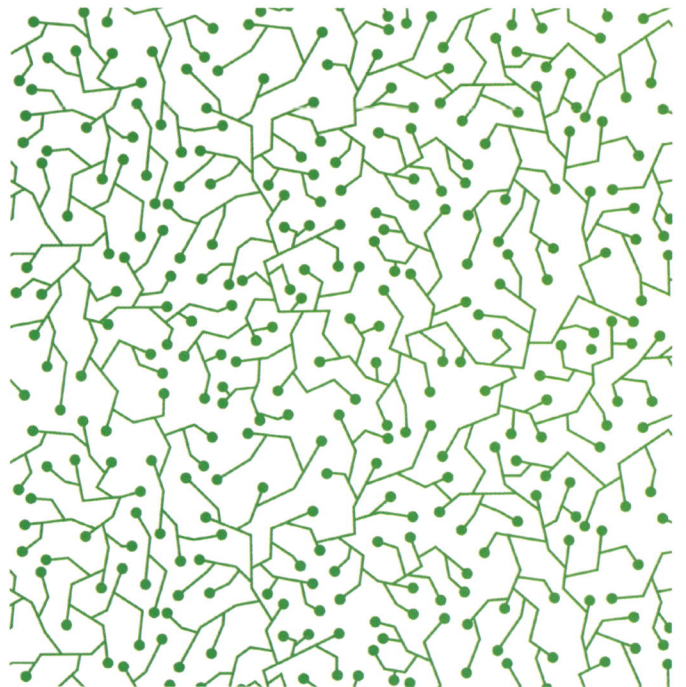

**ALLUMETTE** | Kuboaa collection with Siecle Colours

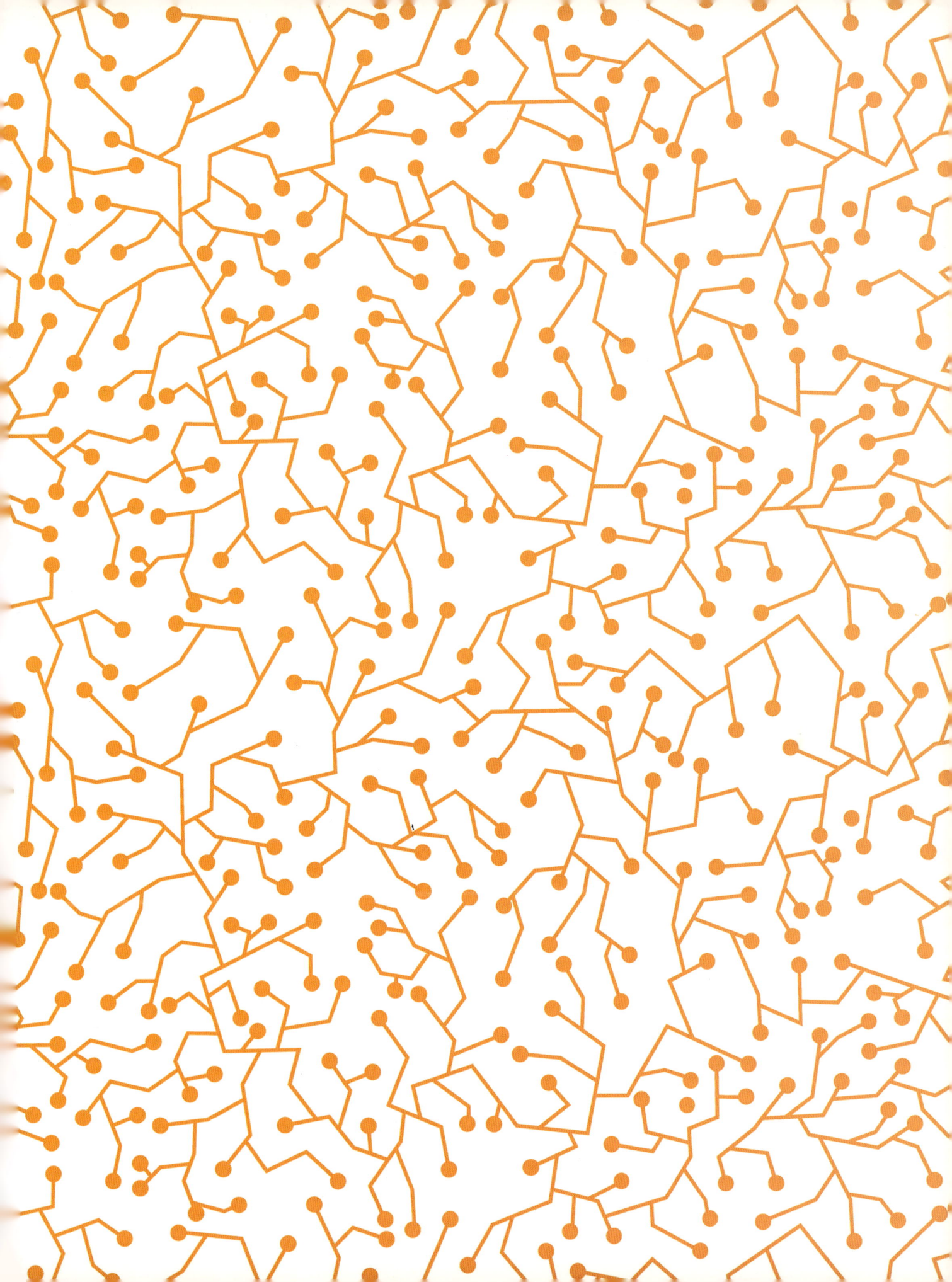

**TWISTING BLOOM** | Kuboaa collection with Siecle Colours

**HUMMING BIRD** | Sofine collection

MODERNS

Tracy Kendall produces her hand-painted wallpaper with subtle elegance and with a contemporary air. This designer has been recognized for the quality of her collections, in which feathers, plants, flowers, and even classic cutlery items, all magnified, have been simplified to give rise to simple, modern designs. Kendall fits within a tendency that pursues the three-dimensional perspective, for which she uses techniques to give the walls innovative textures and forms. Her collection achieves a spectacular visual impact—from isolated pieces used in concrete spaces to general decoration. All the figures have been perfected using a pure approach, and enhance both traditional and contemporary interiors. Her collections can be reproduced in a single color, or printed with a graduated or rainbow effect.

ELLE BUTTONS

CONDOM

AIRHEADS ▶

**OPEN FEATHER** | Feathers collection

**AGAPANTHUS** | Florals collection

**SLIM FEATHER** | Feathers collection

MODERNS

**SKELETON** | Florals collection

**SKELETON** | Florals collection

HEARTWEED | Florals collection

MEDHAREBELL | Florals collection

AIRHEADS | Florals collection

MODERNS

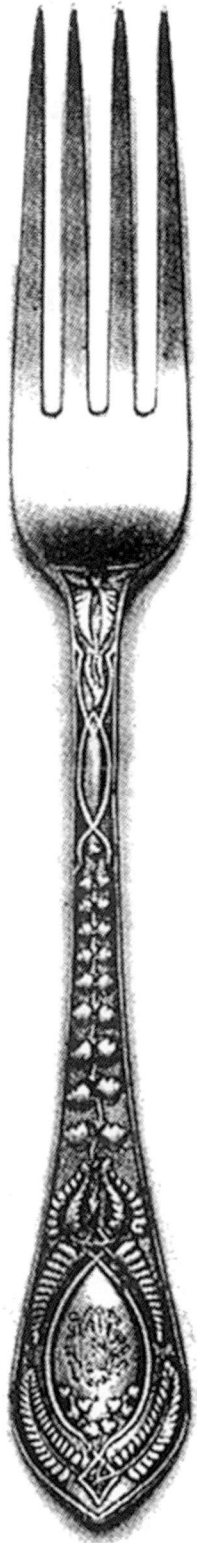

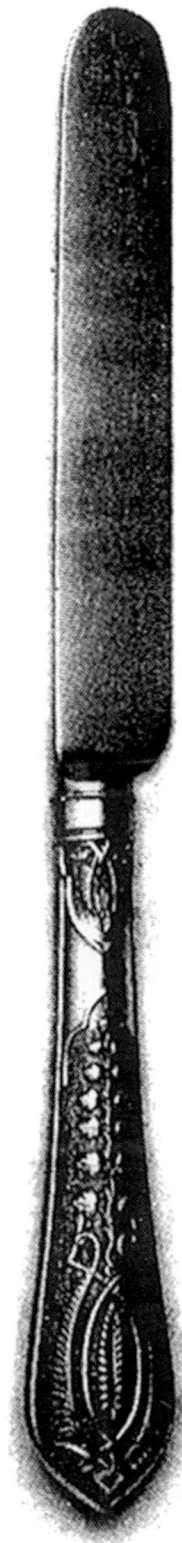

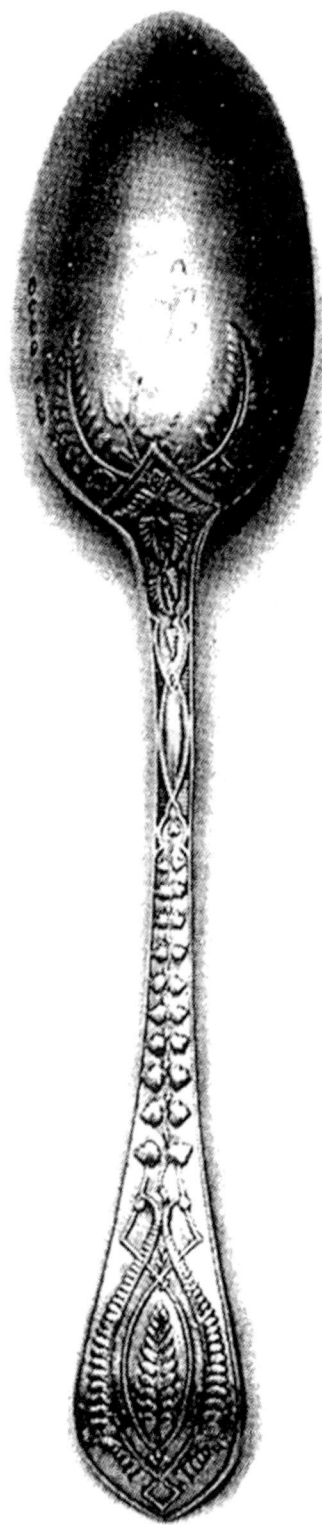

**FORK, KNIFE, SPOON** | Eat collection

BOOKS

MAGAZINES

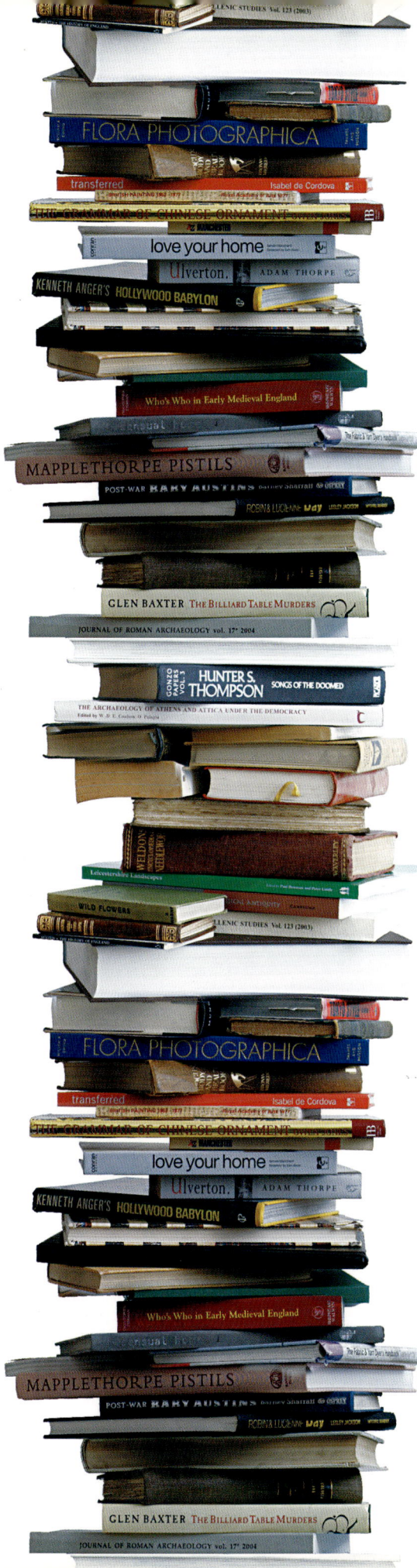

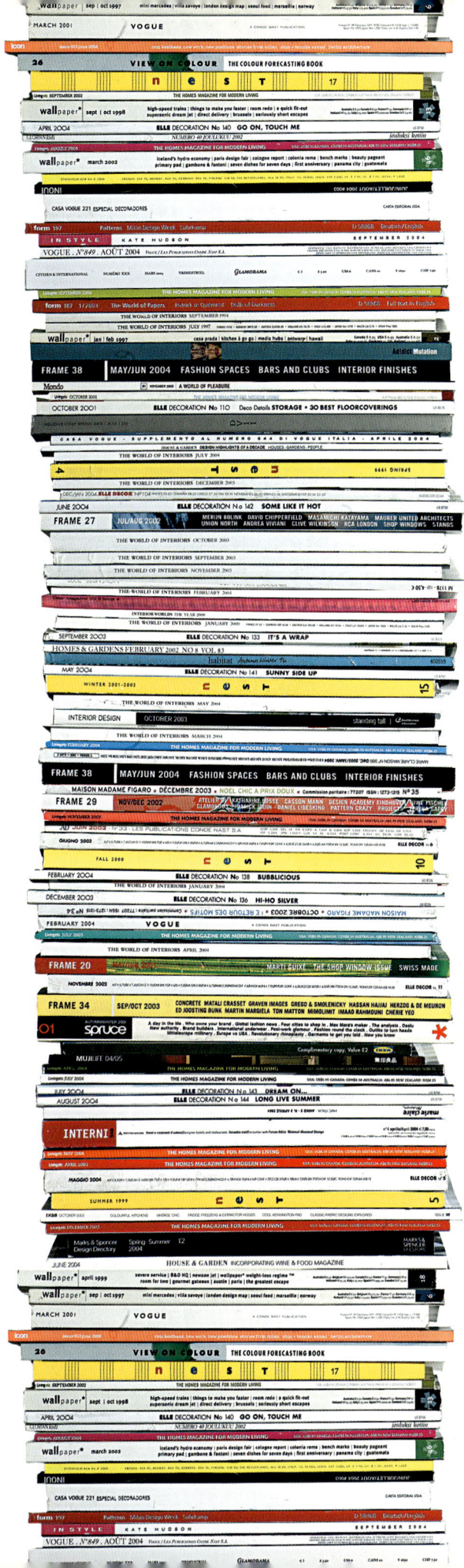

**Left stack (books, top to bottom):**

...LENIC STUDIES Vol. 123 (2003)

FLORA PHOTOGRAPHICA

transferred — Isabel de Cordova

THE GRAMMAR OF CHINESE ORNAMENT — MANCHESTER

love your home

Ulverton. ADAM THORPE

KENNETH ANGER'S HOLLYWOOD BABYLON

Who's Who in Early Medieval England

MAPPLETHORPE PISTILS

POST-WAR MARY AUSTINS

ROBIN & LUCIENNE Day

GLEN BAXTER — The Billiard Table Murders

JOURNAL OF ROMAN ARCHAEOLOGY vol. 17* 2004

GONZO PAPERS VOL.3 — HUNTER S. THOMPSON — SONGS OF THE DOOMED

THE ARCHAEOLOGY OF ATHENS AND ATTICA UNDER THE DEMOCRACY

WELDON

Leicestershire Landscape

WILD FLOWERS

...LENIC STUDIES Vol. 123 (2003)

FLORA PHOTOGRAPHICA

transferred — Isabel de Cordova

THE GRAMMAR OF CHINESE ORNAMENT — MANCHESTER

love your home

Ulverton. ADAM THORPE

KENNETH ANGER'S HOLLYWOOD BABYLON

Marks & Spencer Design Directory

Who's Who in Early Medieval England

MAPPLETHORPE PISTILS

POST-WAR MARY AUSTINS

ROBIN & LUCIENNE Day

GLEN BAXTER — The Billiard Table Murders

JOURNAL OF ROMAN ARCHAEOLOGY vol. 17* 2004

**Right stack (magazines, top to bottom):**

wallpaper* sep | oct 1997 — mini mercedes | villa savoye | london design map | seoul food | marseille | norway

MARCH 2001 — VOGUE

Icon

26 — VIEW ON COLOUR — THE COLOUR FORECASTING BOOK

n e s t — 17

THE HOMES MAGAZINE FOR MODERN LIVING

wallpaper* sept | oct 1998 — high-speed trains | things to make you faster | room redo | a quick fit-out — supersonic dream jet | direct delivery | brussels | seriously short escapes

APRIL 2004 — ELLE DECORATION No 140 — GO ON, TOUCH ME

NUMERO 40 JOULUKUU 2002

THE HOMES MAGAZINE FOR MODERN LIVING

wallpaper* march 2002 — iceland's hydro economy | paris design fair | cologne report | colonia roma | bench marks | beauty pageant — primary pad | gambone & fantoni | seven dishes for seven days | first anniversary | panama city | guatemala

iNONi

CASA VOGUE 221 ESPECIAL DECORADORES

form 197 — Patterns — Milan Design Week — Subkarma

IN STYLE — KATE HUDSON — SEPTEMBER 2004

VOGUE . N°849. AOÛT 2004

CITIZEN K INTERNATIONAL — NUMÉRO XXX — TRIMESTRIEL — GLAMORAMA

THE HOMES MAGAZINE FOR MODERN LIVING

form 187 — The World of Papers — Full text in English

THE WORLD OF INTERIORS SEPTEMBER 2004

THE WORLD OF INTERIORS JULY 1997

wallpaper* jan | feb 1997 — casa prada | kitchen à go go | media hubs | antwerp | hawaii

Mutation

FRAME 38 — MAY/JUN 2004 — FASHION SPACES — BARS AND CLUBS — INTERIOR FINISHES

Mondo — A WORLD OF PLEASURE

THE HOMES MAGAZINE FOR MODERN LIVING

OCTOBER 2001 — ELLE DECORATION No 110 — Deco Details STORAGE + 30 BEST FLOORCOVERINGS

CASA VOGUE - SUPPLEMENTO AL NUMERO 644 DI VOGUE ITALIA - APRILE 2004

THE WORLD OF INTERIORS JULY

SPRING 1999

THE WORLD OF INTERIORS DECEMBER 2003

ELLE DECOR N°104

JUNE 2004 — ELLE DECORATION No 142 — SOME LIKE IT HOT

FRAME 27 — JUL/AUG 2002 — MERIJN BOLINK, DAVID CHIPPERFIELD, MASAMICHI KATAYAMA, MAURER UNITED ARCHITECTS, UNION NORTH, ANDREA VIVIANI, CLIVE WILKINSON, RCA LONDON, SHOP WINDOWS, STANDS

THE WORLD OF INTERIORS OCTOBER 2003

THE WORLD OF INTERIORS SEPTEMBER 2003

THE WORLD OF INTERIORS NOVEMBER 2003

THE WORLD OF INTERIORS FEBRUARY 2004

INTERIOR WORLDS THE YEAR 2004

THE WORLD OF INTERIORS JANUARY 2004

SEPTEMBER 2003 — ELLE DECORATION No 133 — IT'S A WRAP

HOMES & GARDENS FEBRUARY 2002 NO 8 VOL. 83 — habitat

MAY 2004 — ELLE DECORATION No 141 — SUNNY SIDE UP

WINTER 2001–2002 — C U T — 15

THE WORLD OF INTERIORS MAY 2004

INTERIOR DESIGN — OCTOBER 2003 — standing tall

THE WORLD OF INTERIORS MARCH 2004

FEBRUARY 2004 — THE HOMES MAGAZINE FOR MODERN LIVING

FRAME 38 — MAY/JUN 2004 — FASHION SPACES — BARS AND CLUBS — INTERIOR FINISHES

MAISON MADAME FIGARO • Décembre 2003 • NOEL CHIC A PRIX DOUX

FRAME 29 — NOV/DEC 2002 — ATELIER, KATHARINE HISSE, CASSON MANN, DESIGN ACADEMY EINDHOVEN, PATTERN CRAZY

THE HOMES MAGAZINE FOR MODERN LIVING

GRUGNO 2003 — ELLE DECOR

FALL 2000 — C U T — 10

FEBRUARY 2004 — ELLE DECORATION No 138 — BUBBLICIOUS

THE WORLD OF INTERIORS JANUARY 2004

DECEMBER 2003 — ELLE DECORATION No 136 — HI-HO SILVER

MAISON MADAME FIGARO • OCTOBRE 2003 : LE RETOUR DES MOTIFS • N°24

FEBRUARY 2004 — VOGUE

THE HOMES MAGAZINE FOR MODERN LIVING

THE WORLD OF INTERIORS APRIL 2004

FRAME 20 — MAY/JUN 2004 — MARTI GUIXE — THE SHOP WINDOW ISSUE — SWISS MADE

NOVEMBRE 2003 — ELLE DECOR 11

FRAME 34 — SEP/OCT 2003 — CONCRETE, MATALI CRASSET, GRAVEN IMAGES, GREGG & SMOLENICKY, HASSAN HAJJAJ, HERZOG & DE MEURON, ED JOOSTING BUNK, MARTIN MARGIELA, TON MATTON, MIMOLIMIT, IMAAD RAHMOUNI, CHERIE YEO

01 — spruce

MUJILIFE 04/05

THE HOMES MAGAZINE FOR MODERN LIVING

JULY 2004 — ELLE DECORATION No 143 — DREAM ON...

AUGUST 2004 — ELLE DECORATION No 144 — LONG LIVE SUMMER

INTERNI

THE HOMES MAGAZINE FOR MODERN LIVING

MAGGIO 2004 — ELLE DECOR 5

SUMMER 1999 — C U T — 5

EKBO OCTOBER 2003

THE HOMES MAGAZINE FOR MODERN LIVING

Marks & Spencer Design Directory — Spring Summer 2004

JUNE 2004 — HOUSE & GARDEN INCORPORATING WINE & FOOD MAGAZINE

wallpaper* april 1999 — seven service | B&B HQ | newsee jet | wallpaper* weight-loss regime ™ — room for two | gourmet gateaux | austin | paris | the greatest escape

wallpaper* sep | oct 1997 — mini mercedes | villa savoye | london design map | seoul food | marseille | norway

MARCH 2001 — VOGUE

Icon

26 — VIEW ON COLOUR — THE COLOUR FORECASTING BOOK

n e s t — 17

THE HOMES MAGAZINE FOR MODERN LIVING

wallpaper* sept | oct 1998 — high-speed trains | things to make you faster | room redo | a quick fit-out — supersonic dream jet | direct delivery | brussels | seriously short escapes

APRIL 2004 — ELLE DECORATION No 140 — GO ON, TOUCH ME

NUMERO 40 JOULUKUU 2002

THE HOMES MAGAZINE FOR MODERN LIVING

wallpaper* march 2002 — iceland's hydro economy | paris design fair | cologne report | colonia roma | bench marks | beauty pageant — primary pad | gambone & fantoni | seven dishes for seven days | first anniversary | panama city | guatemala

iNONi

CASA VOGUE 221 ESPECIAL DECORADORES

form 197 — Patterns — Milan Design Week — Subkarma

IN STYLE — KATE HUDSON — SEPTEMBER 2004

VOGUE . N°849. AOÛT 2004

GLAMORAMA

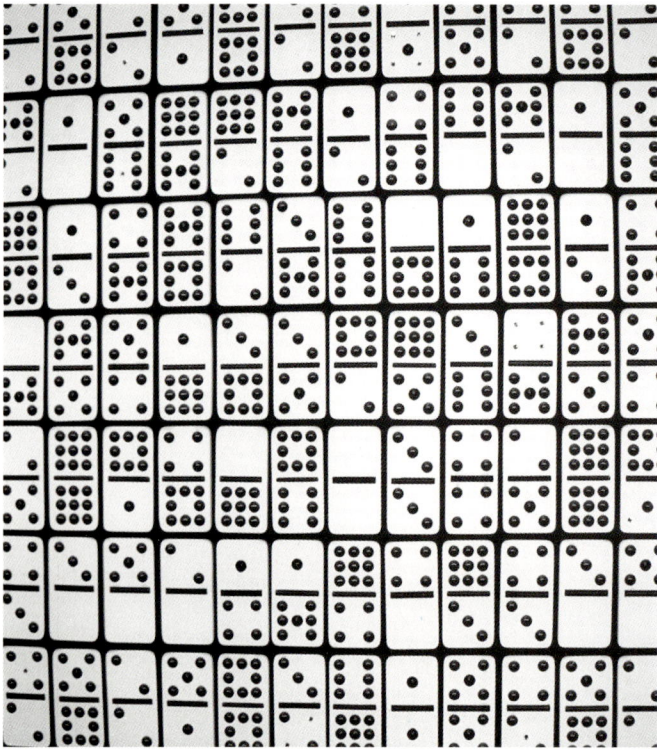

PLATES

MODERNS

DOMINOES ▶

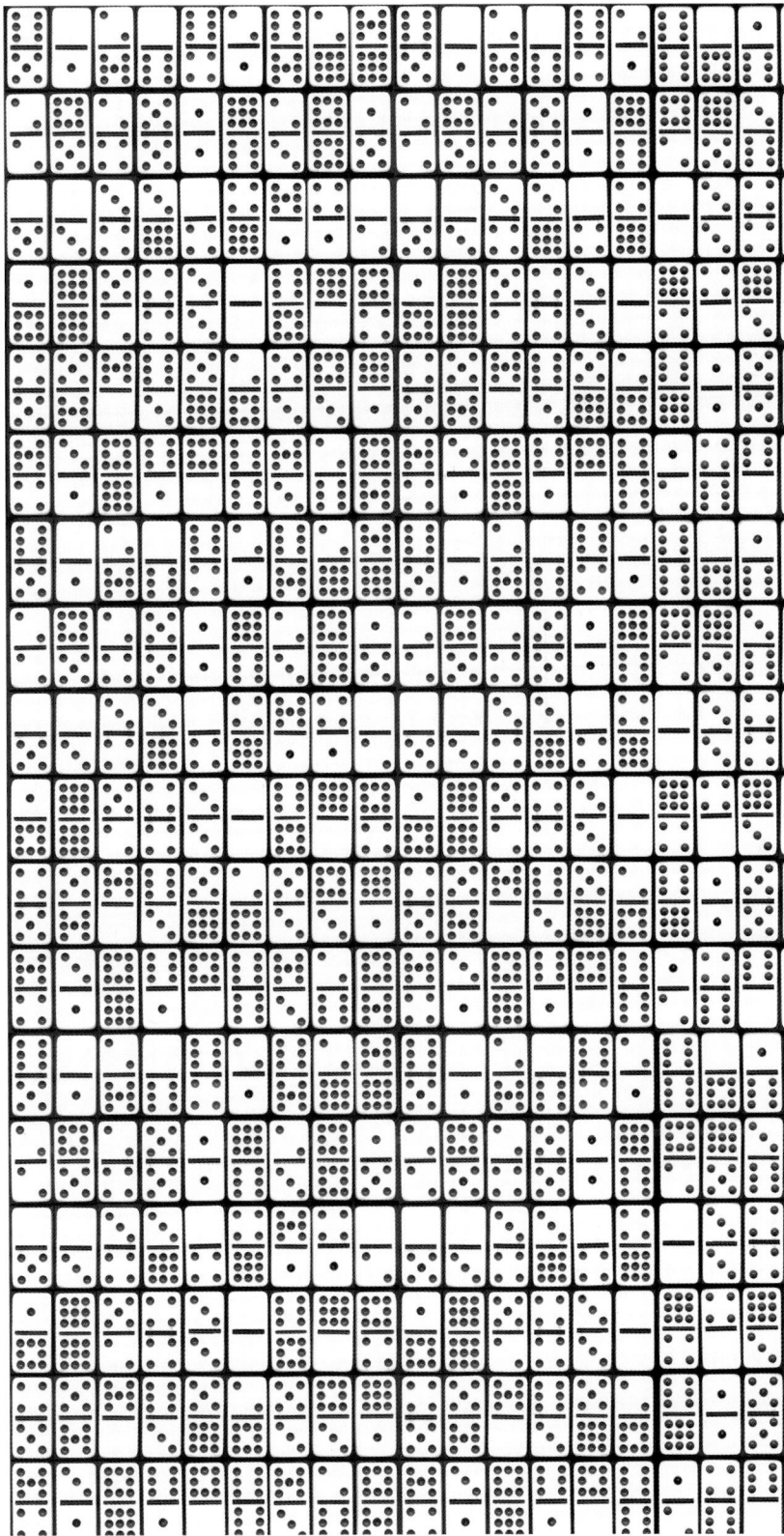

**WHITE CARD** | Stripe collection

MODERNS

WRITING | Stripe collection

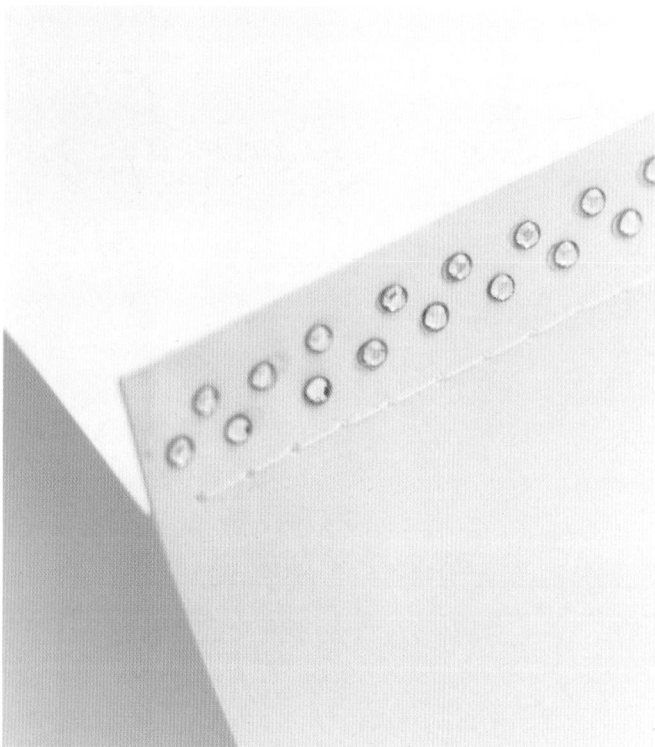

PARIS 2004

PETITDIAMONT | Stripe collection ▶

SEQUINS | Sequins collection

JIGSAW FULL

MODERNS

SHOPPING LIST

BUTTONS

SHOPPING ITEMS

BUTTONS

FLOCK LINES ▶

MODERNS

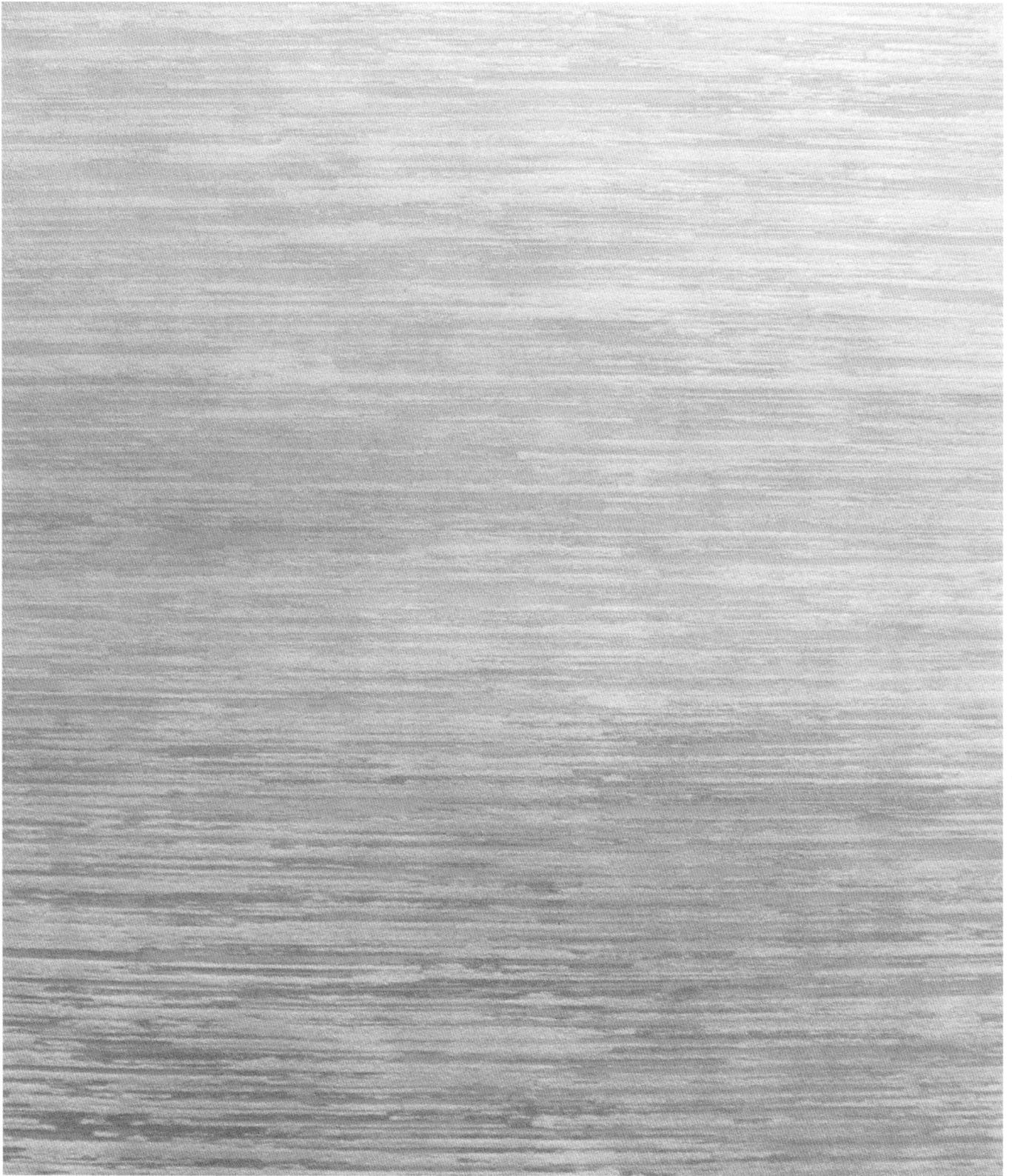

Extratapete, a young German firm based in Berlin, specializes in the design and manufacture of exclusive wallpapers. Thanks to modern production techniques, wallpaper can be manufactured in smaller quantities these days, and this enables the company to offer alternatives with innovative and prestigious prints in a wide range of dimensions to suit the requirements of any space. Its products are ideal both for professional interior designers and for DIY decorating enthusiasts, thanks to the high degree of exclusivity it is able to offer. It even has a specific department that develops personalized designs for professionals in the media, theater, movie house, and art worlds.

BERLIN

PEDRO ▶

YASUMI

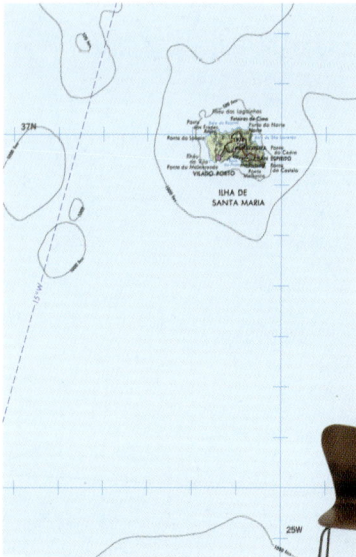

SANTA MARIA

FLORETTA

MODERNS

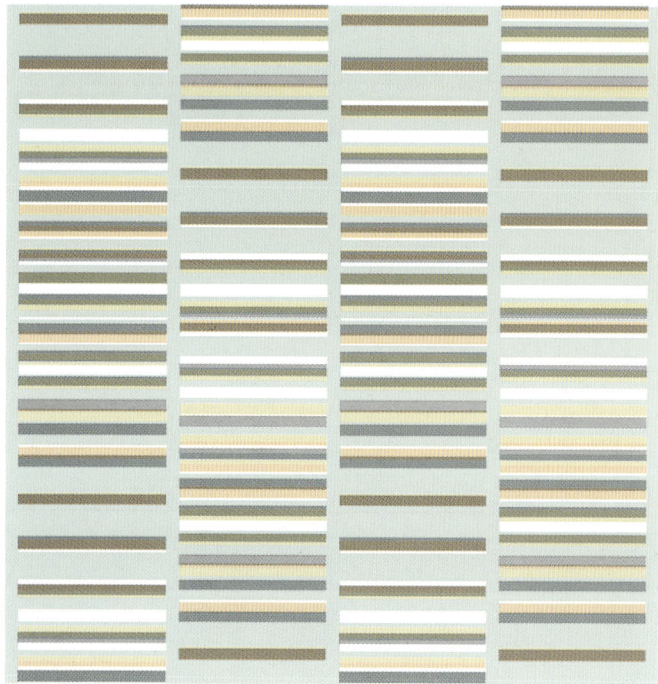

HENRY

MODERNS

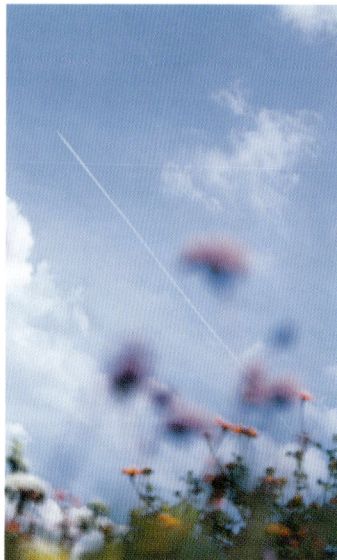

ANABELL

BENITA

BRASILIA

ROSA INGE

SUSANNA

JURI

MODERNS

MARIE

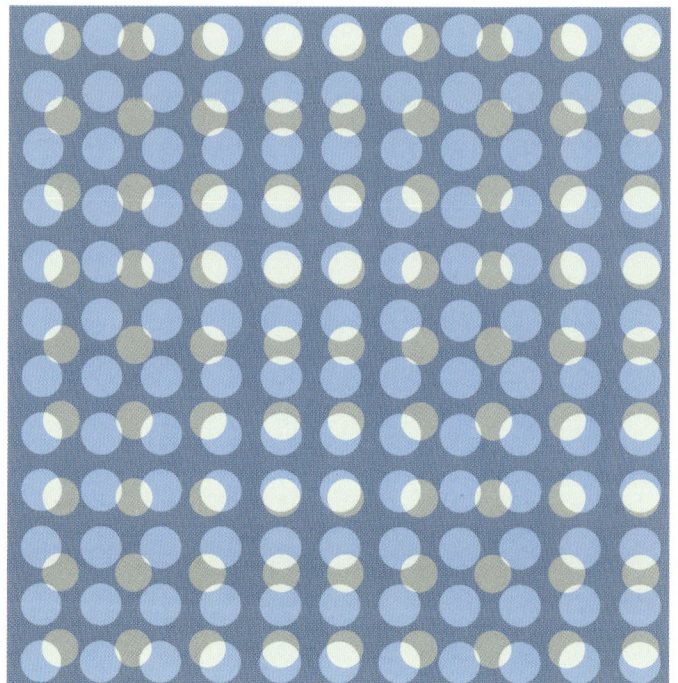

MODERNS

LUI

MODERNS

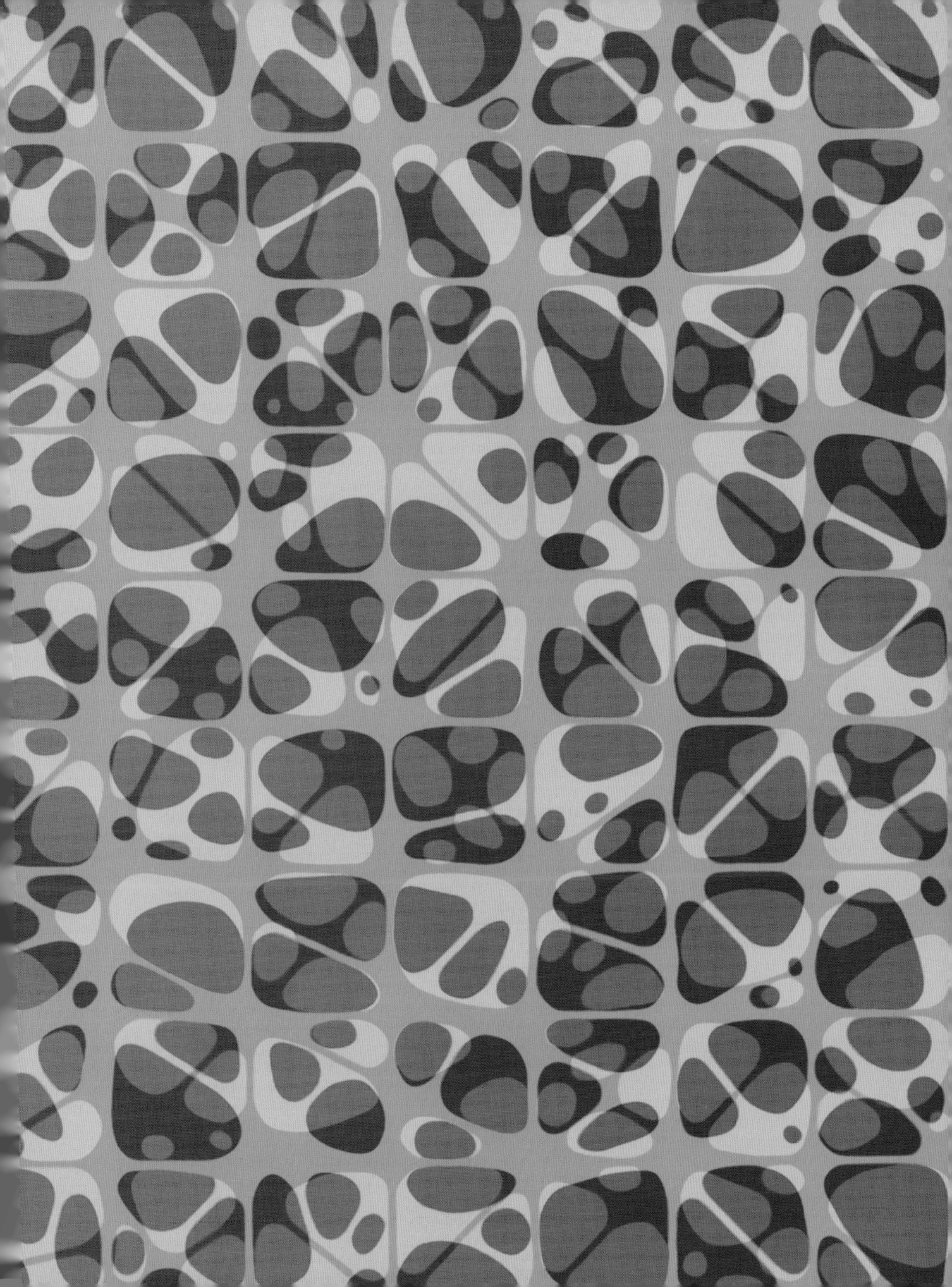

ANNA

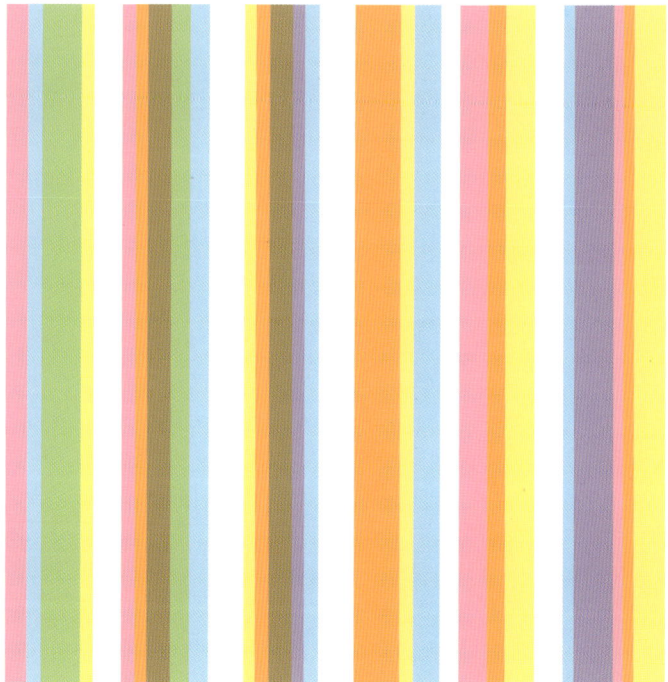

MODERNS

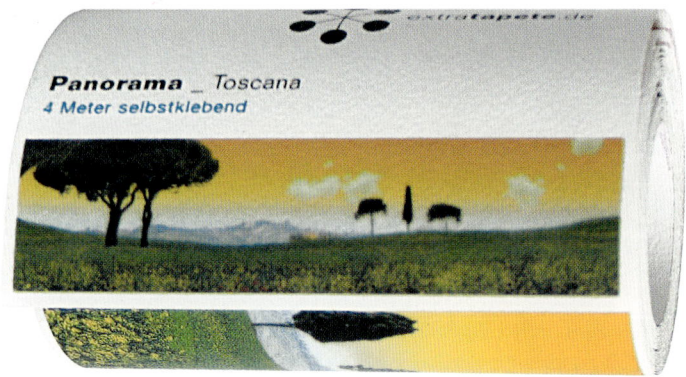

Panorama _ Toscana
4 Meter selbstklebend

TUSCANY

CARIBBEAN

Panorama _ Naturkunde . 4 Meter selbstklebend
Natural history . 4 meter self-adhesive
Science naturelle . 4 mètres autocollant

NATURE

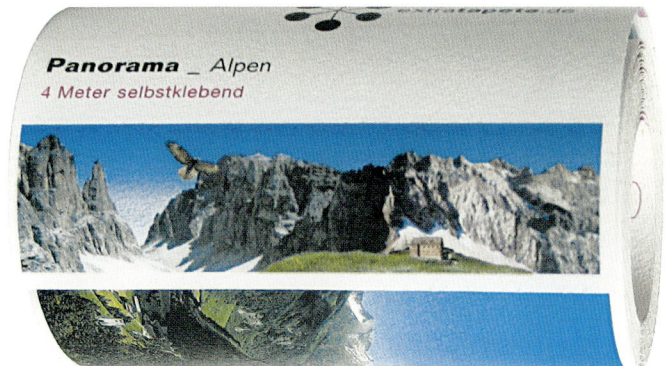

ALPINE

# JOCELYN WARNER

Jocelyn Warner bases her line of decorations on the idea that thousands of images exist in nature that are worth capturing and using to decorate walls. The individual vision of the world that surrounds us is constructed around a connecting theme that knits together a personal and modern collection conceived to form the background of our daily lives. Taking a whole series of organic motifs as her starting point, Warner transforms each of the images into forms with simple lines that, when applied to the wallpaper, configure a series of new interpretations of those images. The prints she employs, together with a careful selection of colors, give the rooms that welcome them a unique air exciting those who seek an individual style for their home. Jocelyn Warner's designs have been recognized throughout the world by a large number of specialist publications.

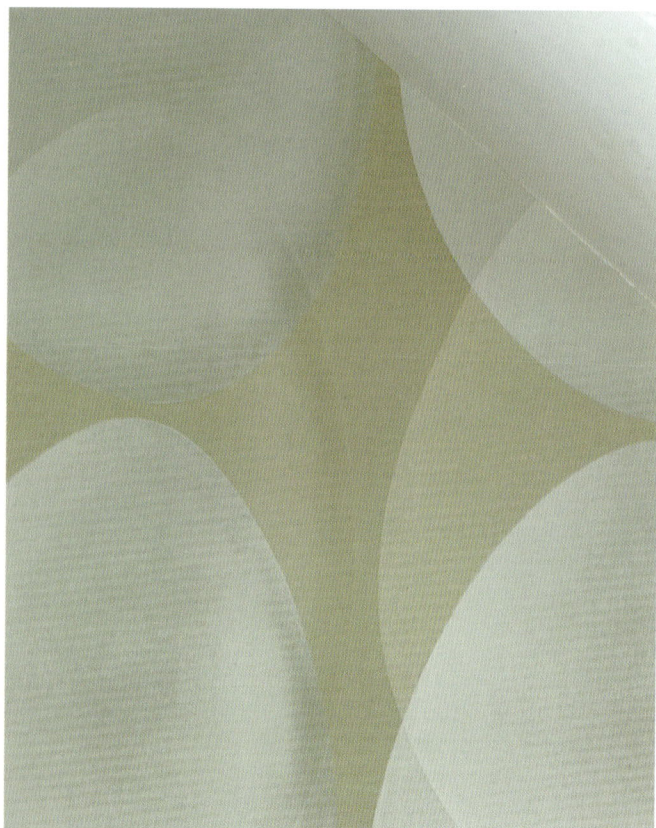

OVAL

LEAF

OVAL

MODERNS

PEONY

MODERNS

LILY

LEAF

KEW

MODERNS

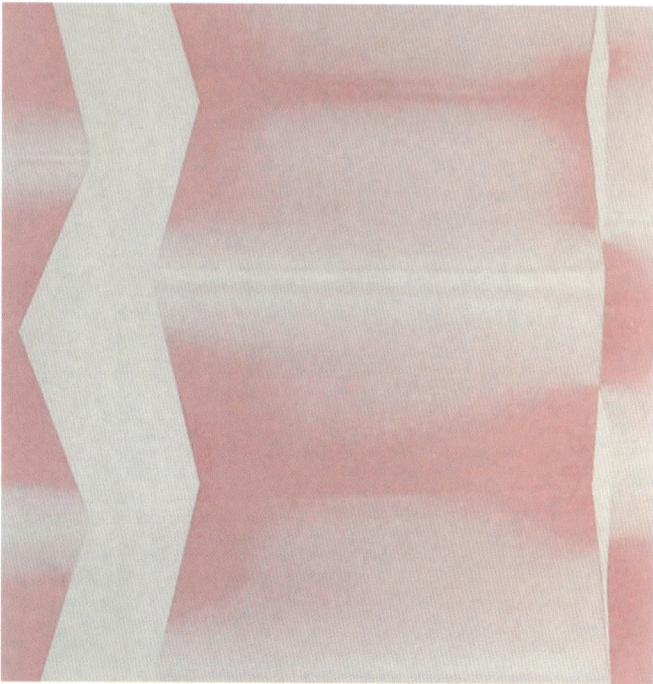

STEP

MODERNS

When designing its wide spectrum of products, Maxalot, founded in 2003, employs a combination of graphic design, iconography, and street art to conceive an image. In the sphere of wallpapers, it has created the Exposif collection, which has been developed in collaboration with important figures in graphic design, photography, and illustration—all of them interested in experimenting in the decoration of interiors. This collection celebrates the renewed importance wallpaper is gaining and champions the idea of modifying a space according to the personal and exclusive criterion of those who reside in it. The collection reflects the changes that wallpaper has recently undergone and demonstrates that it is a protagonist in the progress currently being made in printing techniques.

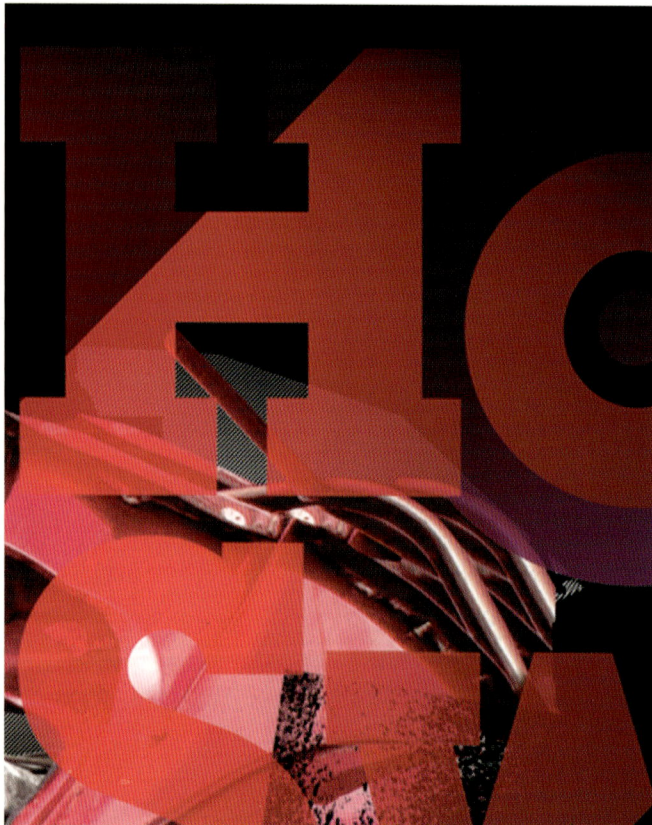

BEETLEBASHER | Design: Jackson Chang

EAGLEMOUNTAIN | Design: Universal Everything

**FROM HELL WITH LOVE** | Design: Phunk Studio

LOVE FOREST | Design: Chisato Shinya/Kinpro

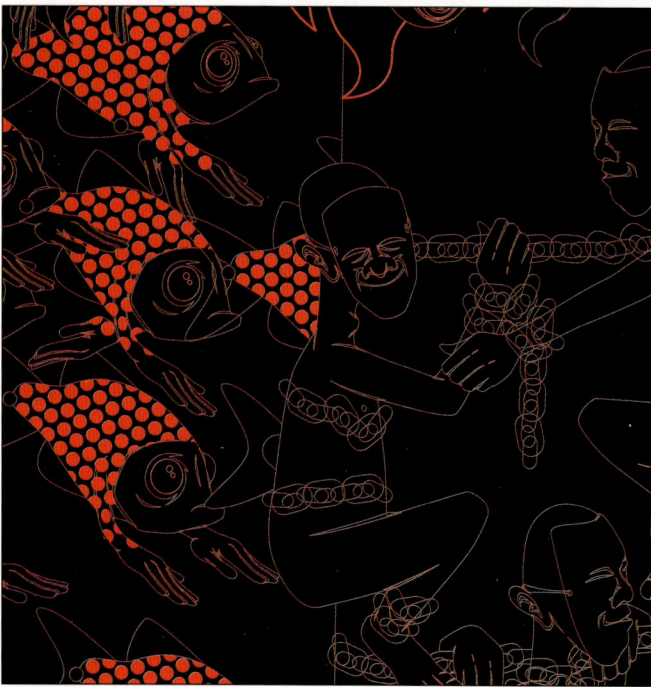

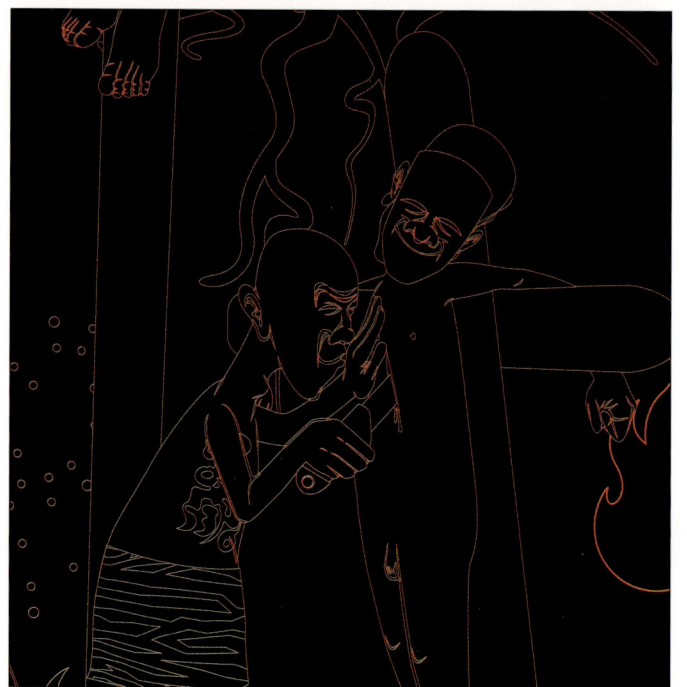

**FROM HELL WITH LOVE** | **Design:** Phunk Studio

UNTITLED | Design: Chisato Shinya/Kinpro

BUY ME | Design: The Designers Republic

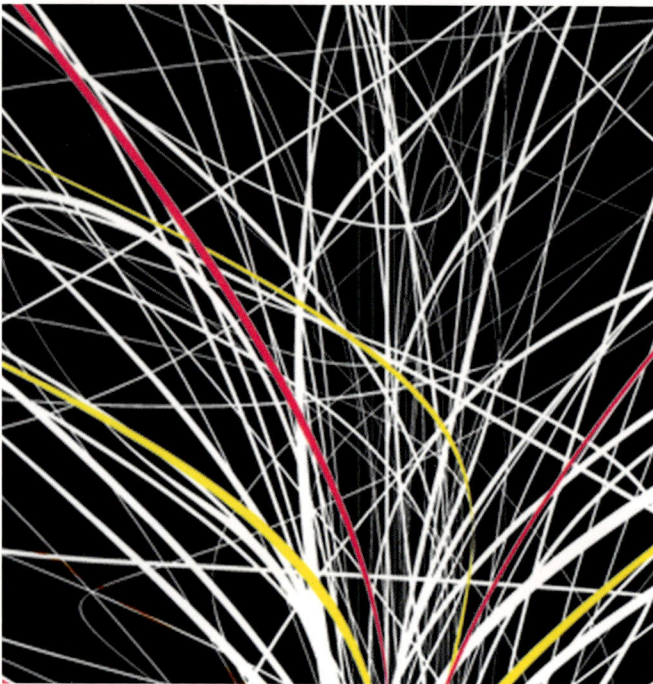

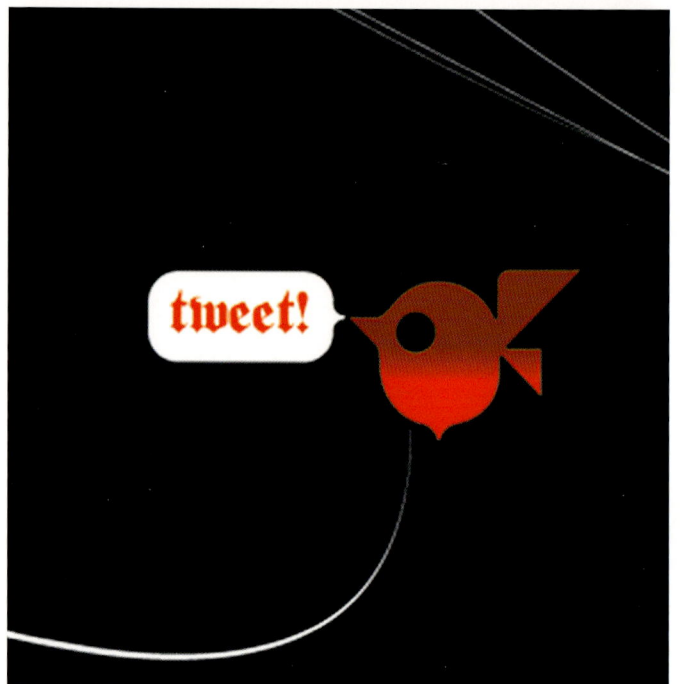

THE SINGING SINGING TREE | Design: Michael Place/Build

MXL_INKA | Design: eBoy

MWP IS YWP | Design: Angel Souto

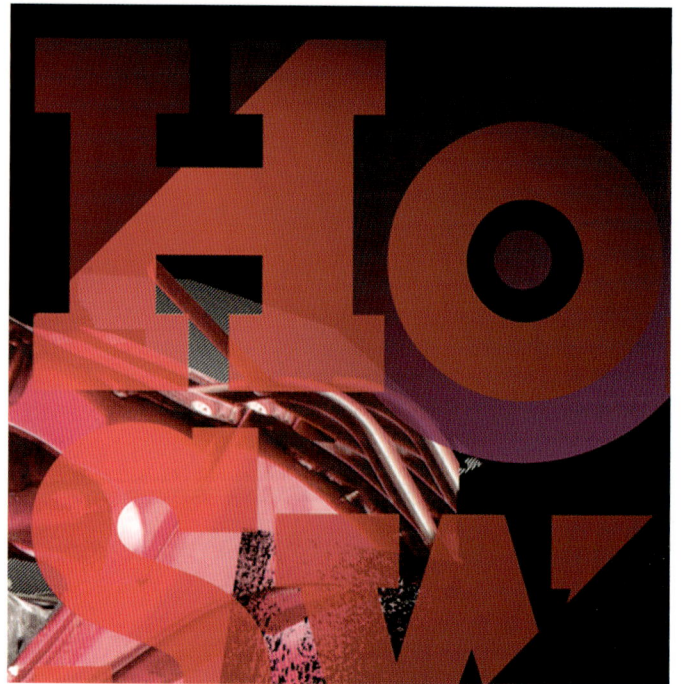

BEETLEBASHER | Design: Jackson Chang

**KNOTTY BY NATURE** | Design: Buck

**FLOW** | **Design:** Kam Tang

**EAGLEMOUNTAIN** | Design: Universal Everything

**ONE TALL TALE** | **Design:** Mike Young/We Work For Them

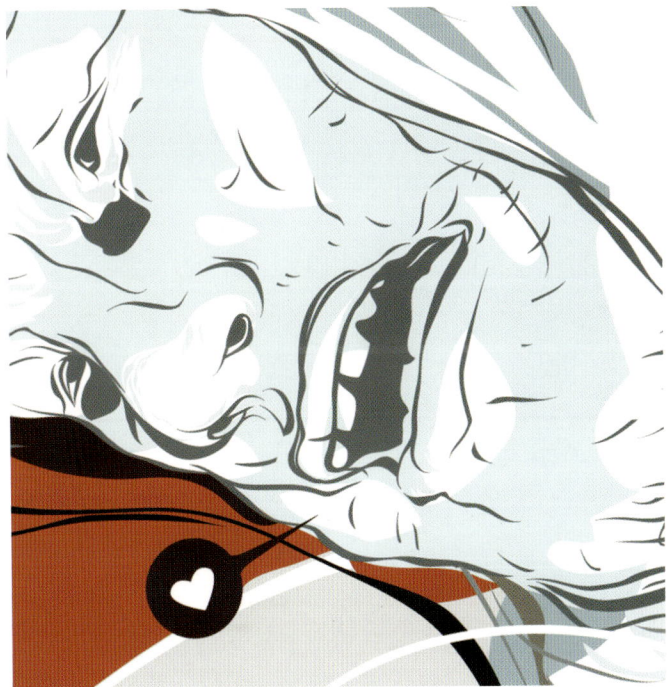

CURRENT | Design: Destroy Rockcity

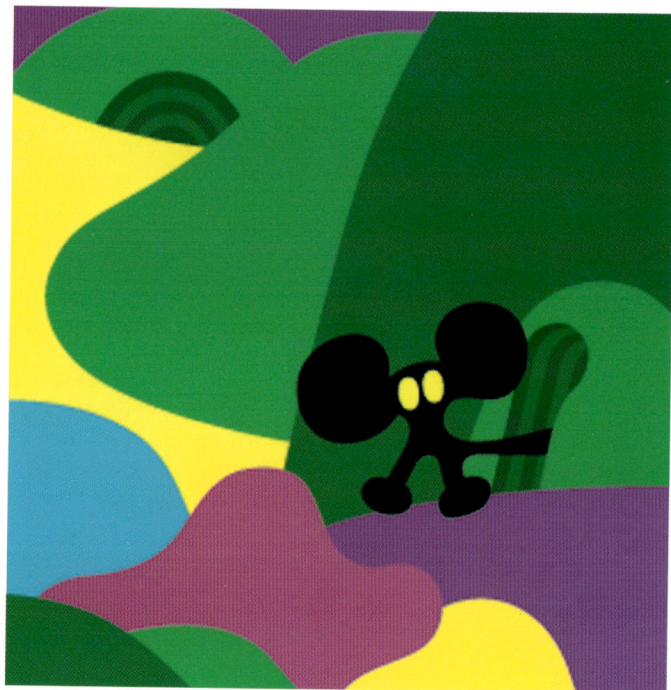

SAMURAI GARDEN | Design: Takora Kimiyoshi Futori

in Liebe zu Deutschland

IN LOVE WITH GERMANY | Design: Kimberly Lloyd & Paul Louis Miller

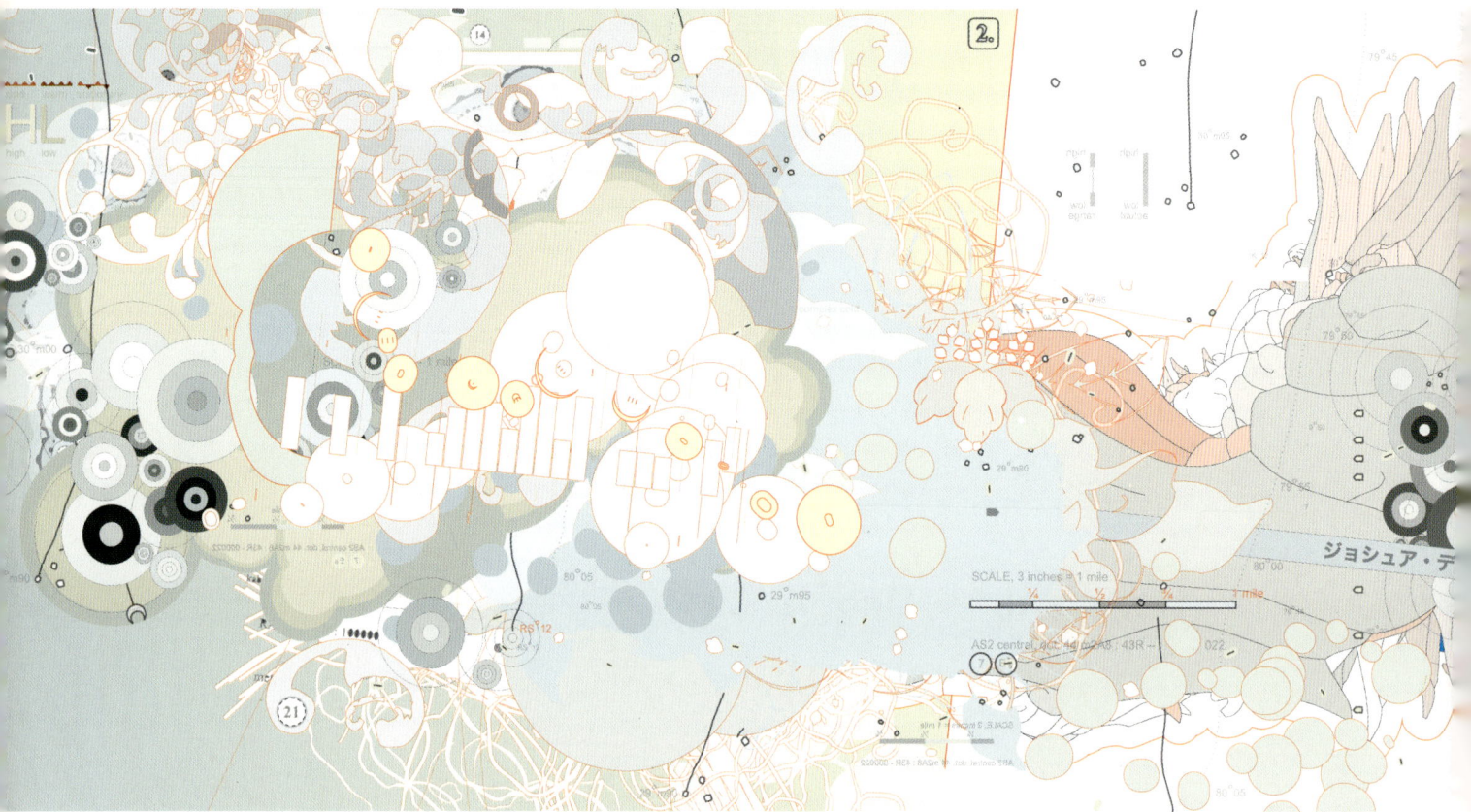

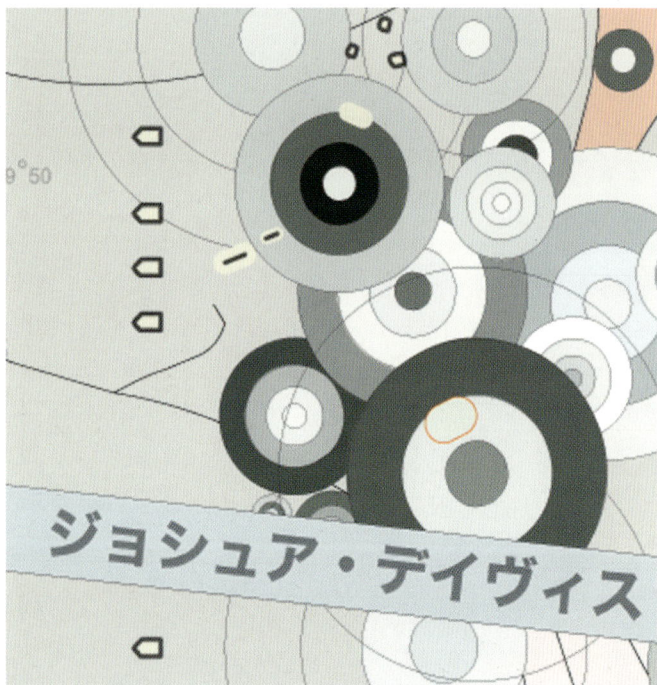

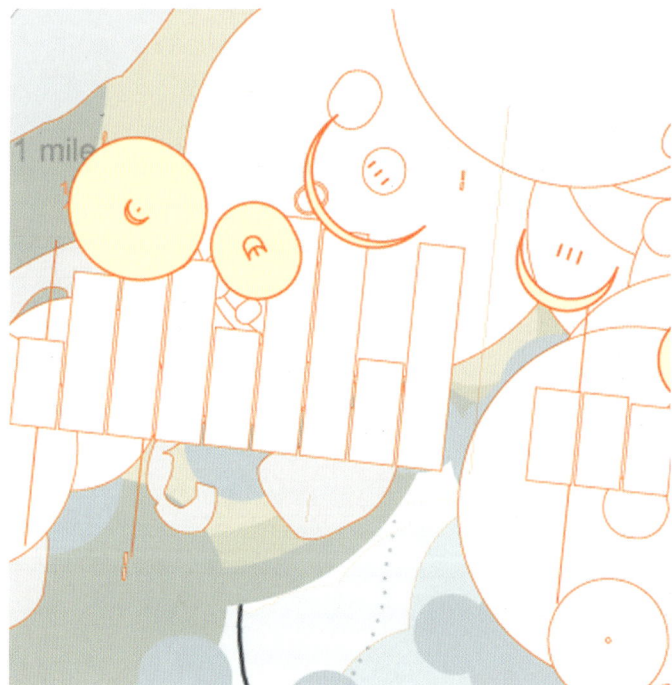

**ONCE UPON A FOREST** | Design: Joshua Davis

ROOM WITH A VUE | Design: Kenzo Minami

**NAVIGATOR OF PARADISE** | **Design:** Erotic Dragon

**DUTCH ELDORADO** | **Design:** Peter Zuiderwijk

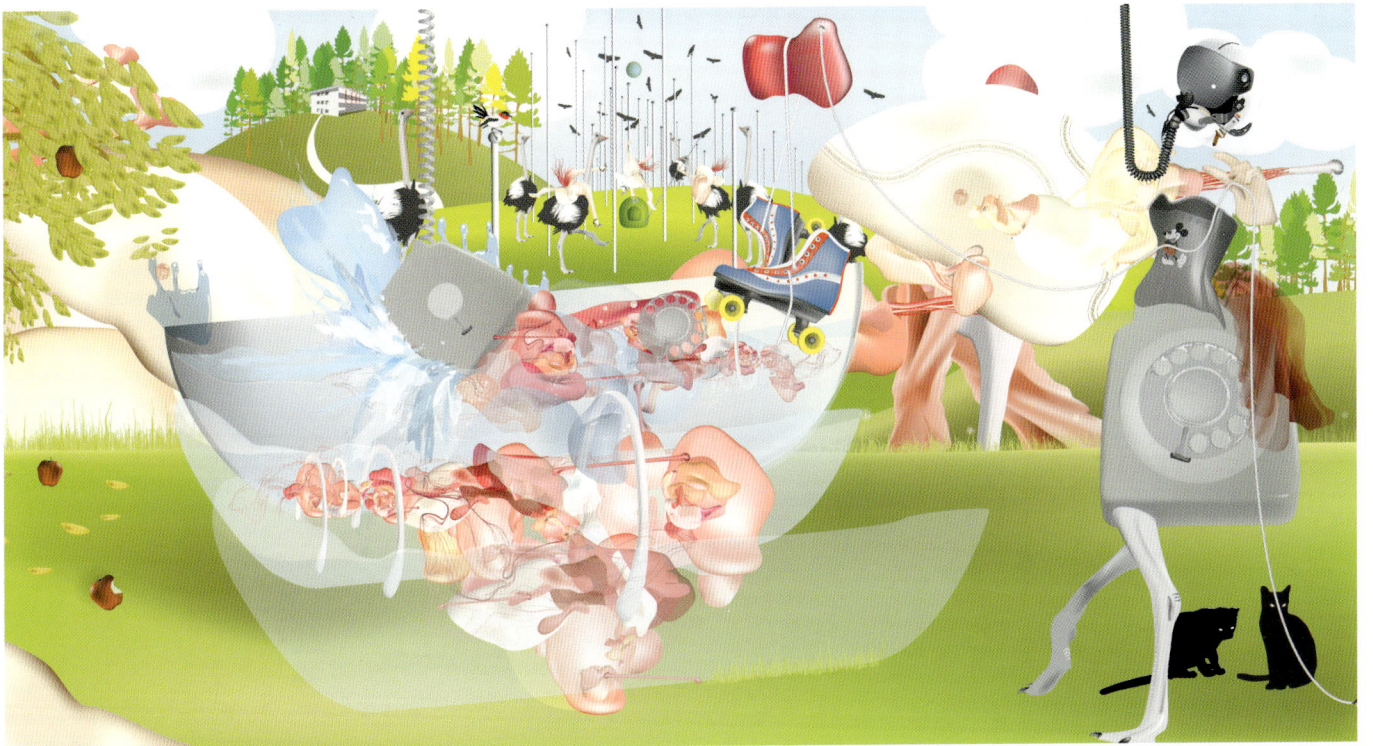

UNTITLED | Design: Pixel Nouveau

FUJI ONE | Design: Pier Fichefeux

**FROZEN HONEY** | Design: Psyop

**TOO MUCH TO DREAM** | Design: Rinzen

**ARCHITYPE WALLPAPER NO. 1** | **Design:** Joshua Davis

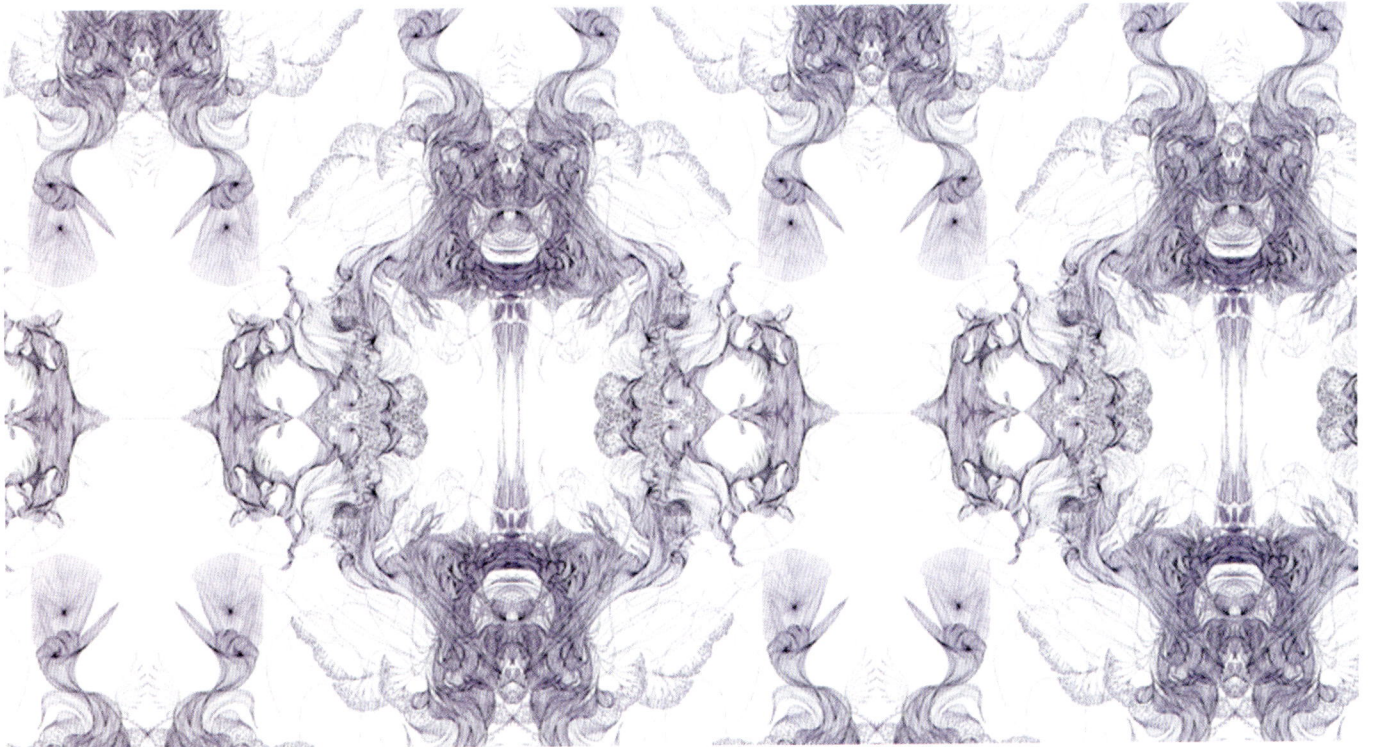

**VOLUTE: PURPLEPATTERN** | **Design:** Florence Manlik

MXL_INKA | Design: eBoy

**FUJI ONE** | Design: Pier Fichefeux

MODERNS

# Classics

In this last section, a whole series of proposals are presented to extend further the variety of wallpapers presented in the previous sections. Here, we focus on a group of prints that are characteristic of the first era of wallpapers, making lavish use of classic themes and motifs. These are connected by a very contemporary current known as Romanticism, based on a revised approach to the style of the same name that emerged in the early 19th century. Those who produce this type of print aspire to decorating warm, inviting environments that favor rest and relaxation without being out of step with the mood of the time.

These motifs confer a great sensation of comfort at the same time as offering the possibility of personalizing the rooms of a home. All that needs to be taken into account are certain basic rules to avoid falling into the trap of overloading a space too much. For example, flat models or those with small motifs convey a sense of space and are easier to combine when choosing fabrics and other ornamental elements, so they are more appropriate in smaller rooms. However, the opposite is true of large prints.

Jane Churchill presents a new collection that reflects the essence of a designer for whom the original illustrations of Beatrix Potter and the Flower Fairies are sources of inspiration. Fresh and relaxing, her designs present stripes edged with delicate lines in pleasant and elegant tonalities or cleverly applied floral motifs that give the room where they are hung a sensation of comfort, elegance, and luxury that are difficult to achieve with other coverings. Churchill concerns herself with all the furnishing accessories a room may need. That is why she includes printed fabrics in her range of products, so drapes, cushions, covers for armchairs and chairs, bed linen, and anything else imaginable can be made to match. Furthermore, she uses a wide variety of other resources to match her fabrics, such as embroideries and velvet for the finishes of some of her pieces.

ASHBROOK COLLECTION | Design: Belview Stripe

ASHBROOK COLLECTION | Design: Kemsley

ASHBROOK COLLECTION | Design: Allenby

CLASSICS

ASHBROOK COLLECTION | Design: Melford

CLASSICS

ASHBROOK COLLECTION | Design: Landsdel ▶

ASHBROOK COLLECTION | **Design:** Chalfield

CLASSICS

ASHBROOK COLLECTION | Design: Dalton

CLASSICS

In Manuel Canovas' products we can easily appreciate the artist's great knowledge of both painting technique and textile making, together with his unquestionable ability to combine the precision of a draftsman with the instinct of a colorist. His style has been recognized internationally for his colors, his exclusive floral prints, and his luxurious fabrics. A garden enthusiast and a passionate traveler, this artist has designed a new collection for the home, a universe of luxuriant flowers, and designs inspired by the experiences he has accumulated in his visits to other countries. Indian art, the perfection of Japanese graphic arts, geometric forms, nature, American folk, and any other situation Canovas encounters can give rise to a new pattern. He supplements his range of products with a bathroom line, another for the table, and also candles and perfumes, to give the home an exotic touch.

Design: Pali

Design: Ange

1. Como Flower; 2. Pali; 3. Nantes; 4. Palme; 5. Como Flower

**TELMA COLLECTION** | Design: Tessa

1. Nantes; 2. Como Flower; 3. St. Barths; 4. Monte-Carlo; 5. Tulipa

TELMA COLLECTION | Design: Nankin

CLASSICS

1. Odin; 2. and 6. Malmo; 3. and 8. Vega; 4. and 5. Kya; 7. Ange

This company has its base in the heart of a Swedish region with a great textile tradition. Its products are directed at a demanding public that loves decoration. Its team works efficiently to create magnificent wallpapers and fabrics the motifs of which are inspired by travel, magazines, old houses, and other experiences from people's lives, which it presents with great harmony in carefully combined collections. Its business concept is based on satisfying its customers' desire to make its dream of enjoying the best in homes a reality. The wallpapers are produced in its own factory with great refinement and care—for example, all the borders are painted by hand—and do not appear on the market until they have undergone strict quality control. In fall 2006, Sandberg launched its first wallpaper collection manufactured with a traditional surface printing method.

EDWARD | Felix & Diana collection ▶

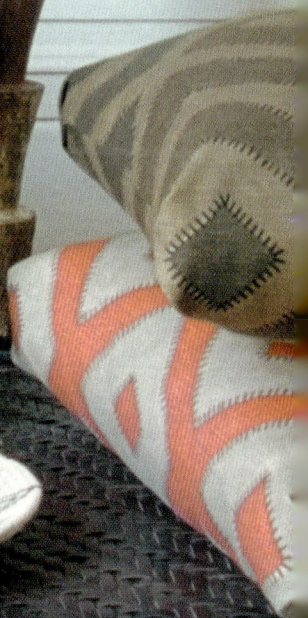

RANOLD & YLVA | Katarina collection

FELIX | Felix & Diana collection

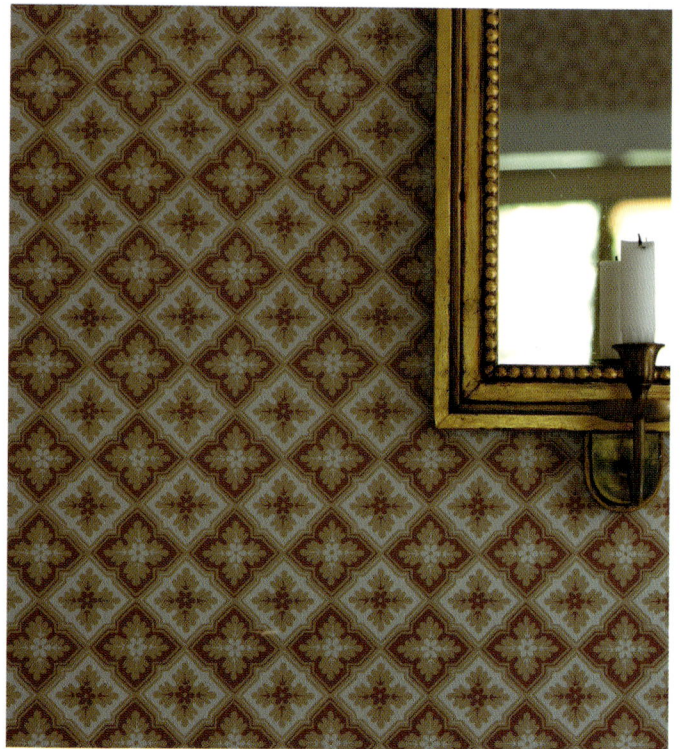

EDVIN & HENRIETTA | Katarina collection ▶

CLASSICS

**JOHN & DIANA** | Felix & Diana collection

**VERA** | Elliot & Alice collection

**VERA** | Elliot & Alice collection ▶

CLASSICS

MAGNUS & CARL-GUSTAF | Ulrika Eleonora collection

ULRIKA ELEONORA | Ulrika Eleonora collection

FREDERIKA | Ulrika Eleonora collection ▶

EDVIN & HENRIETTA | Katarina collection

SIMON | Felix & Diana collection

PONTUS | Pontus & Melker collection

CLASSICS

**WILLIAM** | Ulrika Eleonora collection

CLASSICS

# EIJFFINGER

This Dutch firm designs and manufactures a vast range of drapes, tapestries, and wallpapers. Its collections include both modern and contemporary motifs, and a more classic and romantic style. Its production specializes in wall coverings, whether paper or canvas, often combined with matching textiles in order to create a personalized environment to suit the customer—as is the case with the Happy View collection, with its modern floral and cashmere prints, perfect for true fashion lovers. Other collections that do not enjoy all these accessories are Grand Gala—a wide range of damasks, checks, and other printed ornaments—and Restrospection—inspired by the 1970s. One of this company's most important collections is Wallpower, in which Eijffinger demonstrates that it is viable to cover a wall with a single oversized motif.

RETRO | Retrospection collection

HERE WE ARE! | Wallpower collection

347020 | Retrospection collection ▶

347115 | Black & White collection

347106 | Black & White collection

CLASSICS

PARIS | Happy View collection

CALLIGRAPHY | Wallpower collection

HERE WE ARE! | Wallpower collection

PARIS | Happy View collection

AMALIA | Wallpower collection

HAWAI | Happy View collection

HAWAI | Happy View collection

BRUSSELS | Happy View collection

LONDON | Happy View collection

# Directory

**Claude Closky**
closky.online.fr

**Erica Wakerly**
Studio 5
96 De Beauvoir Road
London N1 4EN, UK
Tel: +44 7940 577620
www.printpattern.com

**Extratapete GbR**
Sredzkistraße 58
D-10405 Berlin, Germany
Tel: +49 30 261 57 29
Fax: +49 30 440 497 56
www.extratapete.de

**Gebr. Eijffinger BV**
Heliumstraat 100
2718 SL Zoetermeer
The Netherlands
Tel: +31 79 344 1200
Fax: +31 79 331 1703
www.eijffinger.nl

**Habitat**
The Heal's Building
22–24 Torrington Place
London WC1E 7LH, UK
Tel: +44 0844 499 1111
www.habitat.net

**Jane Churchill/Colefax Group**
19–23 Grosvenor Hill
London W1X 3QD, UK
Tel: +44 207 318 6000
Fax: +44 207 499 9910
www.janechurchill.com

**Jocelyn Warner**
3–4 Links Yard, Spelman Street
London E1 5LX, UK
Tel: +44 207 375 3754
Fax: +44 207 422 0080
www.jocelynwarner.com

**Johanna Basford Designs**
Mill of Elrick Fish Farm
Auchnagatt, Ellon
Aberdeenshire AB41 8US, UK
Tel: +44 7921 072924
www.johanna-basford.co.uk

**Kuboaa Ltd.**
24 Barton Street
Bath BA1 1HG, UK
Tel: +44 1225 444089
www.kuboaa.co.uk

**Manuel Canovas/Colefax Group**
223 rue Saint Honoré
75001 Paris, France
Tel: +33 1 58 62 33 50
www.manuelcanovas.com

**Markus Benesch**
Mariannenplatz 1
D-80538 Munich, Germany
Tel: +49 89 228 52 62
Fax: +49 89 228 57 14
www.markusbenesch.com
www.moneyformilan.com
www.colorflage.de

**Maxalot**
Palma de Sant Just 9
08002 Barcelona, Spain
Tel: +34 933 101 066
www.maxalot.com

**MoCo Loco**
www.mocoloco.com
This website reviews the contemporary design scene
and new trends.

**Sandberg Tyg & Tapet AB**
Box 69
Hesters Industriområde
523 22 Ulricehamn, Sweden
Tel: +46 321 531660
Fax: +46 321 531661
www.sandbergtapeter.com

**TapetenAgentur**
Jakobstraße 66
D-50678 Cologne, Germany
Tel: +49 221 9328 182
Fax: +49 221 9328 842
www.tapetenagentur.de

**Tracy Kendall**
Tel: +44 207 640 9071
Fax: +44 208 769 0618
www.tracykendall.com

**Tres Tintas BCN**
Aribau 71
08036 Barcelona, Spain
Tel: +34 93 454 43 38
Fax: +34 93 451 45 34
www.trestintas.com

**Veruso**
Rind'sche Stiftstraße 38
D-61348 Bad Homburg, Germany
Tel: +49 6172 6814 20
Fax: +49 6172 6814 21
www.veruso.com

# Photographic credits

Eduard Llasat, p. 20

Duna Riera, pp. 50–64

Joséphine de Bère (courtesy of Editions du Centre Pompidou), pp. 66–67, 70–71

Joséphine de Bère (courtesy of the Galería Laurent Godin), pp. 68–69, 72–77

Colefax Group, pp. 214–228